DIRECTIONS IN DEVELOPMENT

Everyone's Miracle?

Revisiting Poverty and Inequality in East Asia

Vinod Ahuja
Benu Bidani
Francisco Ferreira
Michael Walton

The World Bank
Washington, D.C.

The findings, interpretations, and conclusions expressed in this study are entirely those of the authors and should not be attributed in any manner to the World Bank, to its affiliated organizations, or to members of its Board of Executive Directors or the countries they represent.

Cover photographs by Curt Carnemark, The World Bank.

Vinod Ahuja, Benu Bidani, and Francisco Ferreira are economists in the Poverty Reduction and Economic Management Unit of the East Asia and the Pacific Region at the World Bank. Michael Walton, who was chief economist for the East Asia and the Pacific Region until June 1997, is now the director of poverty reduction in the Poverty Reduction and Economic Management Network at the World Bank.

Library of Congress Cataloging-in-Publication Data

Everyone's miracle? : Revisiting poverty and inequality in East Asia / Vinod Ahuja . . . [et. al.]
p.   cm. — (Directions in development)
Includes bibliographical references (p. 101).
ISBN 0-8213-3979-6
1. Poverty—East Asia   2.   Income distribution—East Asia.
3. Equality—East Asia   4.   East Asia—Economic policy.
5. Poverty—Thailand—Case studies.   I.   Ahuja, Vinod.
II.   Series: Directions in development (Washington, D.C.)
HC460.5.Z9P616   1997
338.95—dc21   97-26454
                                                          CIP

Contents

Foreword

Poverty reduction is development's most important task. Forty years ago most East Asians lived in deep poverty, with desperately low incomes, short life expectancies, low access to schooling, and high vulnerability to adverse shocks. Remarkable growth since then has had an extraordinary effect on reducing poverty in the region. Poverty has fallen because growth has been highly inclusive, with vast expansion in social services and enormous increases in the productivity of and employment opportunities for the poor. Thus many observers—including the World Bank in its 1993 *East Asian Miracle* study—have characterized the East Asian model as one of growth with equity.

This study revisits poverty and inequality in East Asia and the Pacific, guided by two fundamental concerns. First, poverty remains a problem in the region. Although poverty has essentially been eradicated in the four "tiger" economies—Hong Kong (China), the Republic of Korea, Singapore, and Taiwan (China)—about a third of the world's poor still live in East Asia. Most of the region's poor are in countries that have not received sufficient attention, including in *The East Asian Miracle*—Cambodia, China, Lao PDR, Mongolia, the Philippines, and Vietnam (as well as the Democratic People's Republic of Korea and Myanmar, for which we have little data). And while the incidence of poverty has declined sharply in some other countries—Indonesia and Thailand, for example—new issues have arisen about the remaining poor, who may be harder to reach because of their location or because, for various reasons, they missed out on development.

Second, concerns about inequality are growing in the region. In some cases this concern stems from rising inequality, notably in China, Hong Kong (China), Taiwan (China), and Thailand. Inequality has also become a concern in Indonesia, Malaysia, the Philippines, and Vietnam, where evidence of increases in income inequality is less firm. Much of the renewed focus on inequality is driven by concerns that some groups are being left out of development, that globalization and technological change favor better-off and more-skilled individuals, and that the rich have acquired their wealth unfairly.

This study raises issues that form part of the larger agenda of institutional and structural concerns in the region. The development community should continue to explore these issues. East Asia's past successes sometimes lead observers to believe that development has been taken care of. This is by no means the case. Decades of development remain, as well as major challenges. It is my hope that this study will make a valuable contribution to the ongoing debate on the continuing task of development in East Asia and the Pacific.

Jean-Michel Severino
Vice President
East Asia and the Pacific Region

Acknowledgments

We are grateful for inputs and helpful comments from Nisha Agrawal, Shaohua Chen, John Gibson, Joseph Goldberg, Jim Hanson, Stephen Howes, Frida Johansen, Tamar Manuelyan, Richard Newfarmer, Christina Paxson, Nicholas Prescott, Martin Ravallion, Gurushri Swamy, and seminar participants at the World Bank, the Economic Planning Unit in the Office of the Prime Minister of Malaysia, and the Philippines Institute for Development Studies. Special thanks are due to Valerie Kozel for her substantial contribution to the conception of this book, as well as for her thoughtful comments on an earlier version. The book was edited by Paul Holtz and laid out by Glenn McGrath, both with American Writing Corporation.

Introduction

For the past thirty-five years a number of East Asian economies have persistently recorded some of the highest growth rates in the world. Increasingly, evidence has become available to confirm that this growth has been accompanied by improvements in various indicators of social welfare. Poverty, whether measured by the number of people with incomes or expenditures below a certain threshold or by indices more sensitive to intensity or distribution, has been considerably reduced in these economies. Life expectancy at birth, infant mortality rates, and literacy indicators have all improved in tandem (Johansen 1993). Even inequality, not initially high by international standards, seemed to have fallen. The magnitude of these achievements, particularly when debt burdens and poor policies were compromising economic performance elsewhere in the developing world, has understandably captured the interest of analysts everywhere. There has been much talk of an East Asian "miracle," and the World Bank made its contribution to understanding the process, emphasizing its equitable nature (World Bank 1993a).

Despite recent worries about a slowdown in the growth rate of exports, or about the solidity of some financial systems, on the whole East Asian economies continue to grow at impressive rates. Nevertheless, a number of recent developments, as well as the availability of new distributional data, call for a reappraisal of some of our perceptions of poverty and inequality in the region. The first of these developments is the emergence of a number of transition economies in the region—Cambodia, Lao People's Democratic Republic, Mongolia, and Vietnam—that began reforms considerably later than China. Though they are now beginning to move toward market economies and to integrate with their neighbors, these countries share a legacy of economic problems that includes widespread poverty. Poverty reduction is a recent phenomenon in these countries, and in some cases population momentum means that small drops in the head-count index still translate into increasing absolute numbers of poor people. Today a larger portion of the region's poor live in Indochina and Mongolia than ever before. By 1993, for some poverty lines, Vietnam had overtaken Indonesia as home to the second largest absolute number of poor people in the region. As these facts indicate, the cross-country poverty profile in East Asia is changing, and consequently antipoverty policies in transition economies require more attention. This study provides timely data for as large a group of East Asian economies as is possible, and seeks to redress the balance by incorporating Indochina and Mongolia into the scope of analysis.

The second development, illustrated by analysis of household survey data for Thailand, is that although growth has helped lift most of the population above internationally comparable poverty lines, poverty is becoming concentrated in specific areas and associated with specific occupations. While similar analysis that examines changes in the poverty profile over time is not available for other middle-income countries in the region, many observers suggest that this trend is widespread. Identifying the basic characteristics of East Asia's poor—for example, specifying where they live and what they do—is now the most important task facing those who want to contribute toward poverty reduction policies. Poverty profiles contain far more policy-relevant information than aggregate poverty measures, and here we draw on a number of such studies, including World Bank poverty assessments. Despite the diversity of East Asia's economies, a consistent picture arises of poverty as a predominantly rural, agricultural phenomenon associated with low educational attainment.

The third development is an increase in inequality in some East Asian economies. Although the evidence for this is not firm, concern about inequality appears to be widespread. In economies where inequality has actually increased, such as China, Hong Kong (China), and Thailand, the issue is taken seriously and may in some cases be associated with a decline in the rate of poverty reduction. In other countries, including the Republic of Korea and Malaysia, worries about the falling demand for unskilled labor have fueled concern about income distribution, though there is little evidence as yet of increases in inequality. This study summarizes the most recent distributional data available for the region, indicating disparate trends across countries. It briefly discusses the relationship between inequality and growth and suggests that there are reasons for East Asian policymakers to seek to preserve equity as their economies grow.

The book is organized as follows. Chapter 1 briefly reviews recent economic growth in East Asia as background to the analysis of poverty and inequality trends. Chapter 2 presents the available evidence on aggregate poverty trends and the profile of the poor within countries. Chapter 3 presents the evidence on inequality and briefly discusses why this may be of concern. Chapter 4 presents a case study of Thailand, analyzing its poverty profile and inequality dynamics in detail. Chapter 5 summarizes the set of policies that enabled many countries to reduce poverty and asks whether the new developments warrant any policy changes or new initiatives. Chapter 6 contains concluding remarks.

1
Economic Growth in East Asia, 1965–95

E ast Asia is a diverse region, both in terms of where its economies are today and their growth history (table 1.1). The distinction made in the World Bank's *East Asian Miracle* between a first group of four "tigers" (Hong Kong, China; the Republic of Korea; Singapore; and Taiwan, China), a second group of newly industrialized countries (Indonesia, Malaysia, and Thailand), and a third group of others is useful (World Bank 1993a).

Part of the objective of this study is to refocus attention on the third group, the "other" economies, that may have been neglected in the past because of the emphasis various studies put on economic growth. Though the majority of East Asia's population lives in these countries, they were excluded from consideration, for instance, in the *East Asian Miracle* (World Bank 1993a). This group can be subdivided into three groups: China, a transition economy with more than 1 billion inhabitants and, currently, the highest rate of economic growth in the world; the transition economies (except China) of Cambodia, Lao PDR, Mongolia, and Vietnam; and the Philippines and Papua New Guinea.[1]

Hong Kong (China), Korea, Singapore, and Taiwan (China) have enjoyed high growth rates, with per capita gross domestic product (GDP) rising by more than 6 percent a year during 1965–80. As a result they are now upper-middle- or high-income economies, with per capita incomes above $10,000.[2] Korea, which had a GDP per capita lower than that of the Philippines in 1965, has grown by 770 percent in the thirty years since. Hong Kong (China) and Singapore are among the fifteen richest economies in the world, with per capita incomes above $20,000.

Indonesia, Malaysia, and Thailand picked up momentum somewhat later. During 1965–80, with growth rates between 3.5 and 5.0 percent a year, their performance was distinctly less impressive than that of the tigers, yet already superior to that of any other economy in the region for which data are available, and above the developing country average for the period (3.5 percent). Except in Indonesia, their growth rates were even higher during 1980–95. Though their performance was not as stellar as that of the tigers, these economies were still substantially richer in 1995 than they had been thirty years earlier.

3

Table 1.1 East Asian Growth, 1965–95

Economy	Real GDP per capita (1995 PPP dollars) 1965	Real GDP per capita (1995 PPP dollars) 1995	Growth rate, 1965–80	Growth rate, 1980–95	Growth rate, 1990–95
Hong Kong, China	4,843	26,334	6.2 (6.3)	5.1 (5.3)	4.9 (5.0)
Singapore	2,678	23,350	8.5 (9.3)	6.5 (6.6)	7.4 (6.8)
Taiwan, China	2,324	15,191	7.5 (4.5)	6.3 (4.9)	5.7 (5.2)
Korea, Rep. of	1,528	13,269	6.8 (7.4)	7.5 (7.5)	6.5 (6.6)
Malaysia	2,271	9,458	3.6 (5.6)	4.2 (4.1)	6.0 (2.1)
Thailand	1,570	6,723	4.6 (4.4)	6.4 (5.5)	6.8 (6.3)
Indonesia	817	3,346	4.8 (5.1)	4.4 (4.5)	5.4 (4.8)
China	771	2,749	n.a. (3.5)	8.4 (5.1)	10.8 (9.2)
Philippines	1,736	2,475	2.9 (2.8)	–0.4 (–0.4)	0.1 (0.1)
Papua New Guinea	2,079	2,287	–1.5[a] (0.3)	1.0 (0.4)	5.0 (5.9)
Lao PDR	n.a.	2,171	n.a.	2.2[b] (n.a.)	3.2 (3.2)
Vietnam	n.a.	1,308	-0.8[c] (n.a.)	4.7[d] (n.a.)	5.8 (n.a.)
Mongolia	n.a.	n.a.	n.a.	1.2 (n.a.)	–3.7 (n.a.)

n.a. Not available.
Note: GDP per capita figures are in 1995 purchasing power parity (PPP) dollars. To arrive at the 1995 PPP numbers, Penn World Tables version 5.6 data were updated to 1995 using real growth rates from the countries' national accounts and the U.S. dollar consumer price index between 1992 and 1995 (see Summers and Heston 1991 for a description of the Penn World Tables). Growth rates are average annual rates in real GDP per capita from the national accounts, expressed in local currencies. Figures in parentheses are growth rates in real GDP per capita from the Penn World Tables. The differences between these two reflect changes in the estimated PPP exchange rates over the period. While the figures from national accounts, in domestic currency, can be expected to be better indicators of actual growth performance, the PPP growth rates are included for consistency with the GDP per capita figures.
a. 1973–80.
b. 1985–95.
c. 1965–75.
d. 1986–95.
Source: World Bank data.

China is perhaps an even more dramatic example of increased growth momentum. While its performance in the late 1960s and the 1970s was not much better than average, the economic reforms of 1978–79 and the early 1980s changed all that. At 8.4 percent a year, China had the region's highest average growth rate during 1980–95, and growth continued to accelerate in the 1990s (see table 1.1).

The growth history of the East Asian transition economies is less well known. In fact, a paucity of intertemporally comparable national accounts data prevents us from going back as far as 1965 in at least two cases, Lao PDR and Mongolia. Still, some interesting facts can be discerned. The first is that this group is still heterogeneous, so it may be best to subdivide it into Indochina and Mongolia. Though Lao PDR and Vietnam have recorded much more modest gains than China, they too saw growth accelerate in the 1980s. With growth averaging 5.8 percent a year in 1990–95, Vietnam grew faster than Hong Kong (China) or Indonesia. Mongolia, in contrast, has seen a sharp, accelerating economic decline since data became available, reminiscent of the transitional path of countries of the former Soviet Union. Given its history and geography, this is not surprising. Mongolia was highly dependent on the Soviet trading system. The Soviet Union's collapse in the early 1990s, as well as Russian moves to charge world prices for its oil and other goods, have contributed substantially to Mongolia's economic decline.

Apart from Mongolia and the Philippines, however, there is no question that economic growth in the region, already impressive in 1965–80, has continued at a remarkable pace and become more geographically widespread since 1980. Even Papua New Guinea, whose performance was well below the regional average in the decades preceding the 1990s, achieved 5 percent average annual growth in 1990–95.

2
Poverty in East Asia, 1975–95

We base our initial discussion of poverty levels and trends in East Asia on table 2.1. These estimates, though imperfect, point to important trends in the region's poverty profile, both within and across countries.

Levels and Trends

The estimates in table 2.1 are based on the international poverty line of $1 a day per capita at 1985 prices. This poverty line was originally used in the World Bank's *World Development Report 1990* (World Bank 1990b)

Table 2.1 Poverty in East Asia, 1975–95

Economy	Number of people in poverty (millions)			
	1975	*1985*	*1993*	*1995*
East Asia[a]	716.8	524.2	443.4	345.7
East Asia excluding China	147.9	125.9	91.8	76.4
Malaysia	2.1	1.7	< 0.2	< 0.2
Thailand	3.4	5.1	< 0.5	< 0.5
Indonesia	87.2	52.8	31.8	21.9
China	568.9[b]	398.3	351.6	269.3
Philippines	*15.4*	17.7	17.8	17.6
Papua New Guinea	n.a.	*0.5*	n.a.	1.0[c]
Lao PDR[d]	n.a.	2.2	2.2	*2.0*
Vietnam	n.a.	44.3 [e]	37.4	31.3
Mongolia	n.a.	*1.6*	n.a.	1.9

n.a. Not available.
Note: All numbers in this table (except for Lao PDR) are based on the international poverty line of $1 per person per day at 1985 prices. Italics are explained in appendix A.
a. Includes only those economies presented in the table.
b. Data are for 1978 and apply to rural China only.
c. Data are for 1996.
d. Available data on purchasing power parity (PPP) exchange rates and various price deflators for Lao PDR are not very reliable and lead to anomalous results. Poverty estimates for Lao PDR are based on the national poverty line, which is based on the level of food

and proposed by Ravallion, Datt, and van de Walle (1991), where its rationale is documented.[3] The estimates in table 2.1 are derived from grouped data originating from household surveys. Whenever the distribution for the years in the table was not available, we used the distribution for the closest available year but adjusted the distribution mean by using the average annual growth rate of consumption from the two closest household surveys. For economies for which only one household survey was available, the average annual growth rate of per capita private consumption from national accounts was used to scale the mean. All income and expenditure figures were deflated to 1985 prices and converted to "international" dollars using 1985 purchasing power parity exchange rates from Summers and Heston (1991). For more information on methodology and data, see appendix A, and for conceptual issues in defining and measuring poverty, see box 2.1.

In addition to the inevitable sampling and measurement errors in the original surveys, readers should be aware that the procedures designed to make international comparisons possible themselves introduce uncertainty. This includes errors in estimating "real" purchasing power parity exchange rates and in estimating parametric fits

Head-count index (percent)				Poverty gap (percent)			
1975	1985	1993	1995	1975	1985	1993	1995
57.6	37.3	27.9	21.2	n.a.	10.9	8.4	6.4
51.4	35.6	22.7	18.2	n.a.	11.1	6.0	4.6
17.4	10.8	< 1.0	< 1.0	5.4	2.5	< 1.0	< 1.0
8.1	10.0	< 1.0	< 1.0	1.2	1.5	< 1.0	< 1.0
64.3	32.2	17.0	11.4	23.7	8.5	2.6	1.7
59.5[b]	37.9	29.7	22.2	n.a.	10.9	9.3	7.0
35.7	32.4	27.5	25.5	10.6	9.2	7.3	6.5
n.a.	15.7	n.a.	21.7[c]	n.a.	3.7	n.a.	5.6[c]
n.a.	61.1	46.7	41.4	n.a.	18.0	11.5	9.5
n.a.	74.0[e]	52.7	42.2	n.a.	28.0[e]	17.0	11.9
n.a.	85.0	n.a.	81.4	n.a.	42.5	n.a.	38.6

consumption that yields an energy level of 2,100 calories a person per day and a nonfood component equivalent to the value of nonfood spending by households who are just capable of meeting their food requirements (see World Bank 1995a for details). While the $1 a day poverty line is based on characteristic poverty lines in low-income countries that have comparable food and nonfood consumption needs, this is a different methodological approach than that used for the rest of the economies in the table. Thus the poverty estimates for Lao PDR are not strictly comparable to those for other economies.
e. Preliminary estimate from Dollar and Litvack forthcoming.
Source: World Bank staff estimates.

Box 2.1 Measuring Poverty

Though most people have an intuitive understanding of what is meant by poverty, there is a large, sometimes controversial, literature on how it should be defined and measured. Many analysts have called for a broad approach to living standards that would take into account not only income and access to marketed goods and services but also access to publicly provided commodities, environmental public goods, leisure, and even social capital. These are important determinants of an individual's capabilities, which, it has been argued, should be the focus of welfare analysis (Sen 1981 and 1985). Although most practitioners favor such an approach in principle, data limitations have often forced them to measure poverty by focusing on income or expenditure, which reflect only the contribution of marketed goods and services to welfare.

As an indicator, consumption expenditure is increasingly preferred to income. Not only is expenditure a better guide to an individual's or household's permanent income—the expected value of its average lifetime purchasing power—but income measures, it is thought, are much more subject to error (Deaton 1997; Chauduri and Ravallion 1994). This study uses household expenditure per capita as the welfare indicator whenever possible.[1]

Once survey data on household consumption expenditures are available, the usual procedure is to stipulate an expenditure threshold—the poverty line—below which people are considered poor. Poverty lines can be relative to the country's average living standards, in which case they are usually a fixed proportion of median or mean income, or absolute, in which case they are usually the cost of a minimum bundle of commodities providing for basic nutrition and some nonfood goods (Ravallion 1994).

Once a poverty line has been chosen, most measures concentrate only on the welfare of those with expenditures below it. Thus the poverty line identifies the poor. A popular approach used to aggregate information about the poor in a society is to list three members of the - Foster-Greer-Thorbecke parametric class of decomposable poverty measures, given by

$$P(\alpha) = \frac{1}{n} \sum_{i=1}^{n} \left[\max\left(\frac{z - y_i}{z}, 0\right) \right]^{\alpha}.$$

When $\alpha = 0$, P is simply the head-count. When $\alpha = 1$ it is the normalized poverty deficit (or poverty gap), which gives the product of the head-count and the average distance between the income of the poor and the poverty line. When $\alpha = 2$ it is the poverty severity index. In it, the gaps between income and poverty line are squared—or weighed by themselves—which makes the measure more sensitive to the largest gaps, and hence to the poorest people (Foster, Greer, and Thorbecke 1984). Because of space constraints, we present only the first two of these in table 2.1.

for Lorenz curves from grouped data. The figures reported in table 2.1 may have large standard errors associated with them; hence their sole legitimate purpose is to suggest orders of magnitude and general trends.

Nevertheless, some trends are so pronounced that there is little room for doubt about them. First, poverty reduction in East Asia over the past two decades has been remarkable. The regional head-count index with respect to the constant (1985 prices) $1 a day poverty line was reduced by two-thirds in 1975–95: while six out of ten East Asians lived in absolute poverty in 1975, roughly two in ten did in 1995. Because populations continued to grow, these proportional drops translate into a halving of the absolute number of poor people in the region, from 720 million to 345 million. Further, the rate of decline accelerated over the past decade: whereas the total number of people in poverty fell by 27 percent in 1975–85, the decline in 1985–95 was closer to 34 percent. This pace of poverty reduction was faster than in any other region of the developing world and, as a result, the share of the world's poor living in East Asia has been declining. This trend is noticeable even in a short (six-year) interval: whereas the region's share was 38 percent in 1987, it had fallen below 34 percent by 1993, the latest year for which comparable data are available for other regions (figure 2.1).

Within East Asia neither poverty levels nor rates of decline were identical across countries. In 1975 China and Indonesia contained 92 percent of the region's poor, largely because they were the two most populous countries. Since 1975, however, both countries have recorded substantial declines in poverty—82 percent in Indonesia and 63 percent

Figure 2.1 Distribution of World's Poor, 1987 and 1993

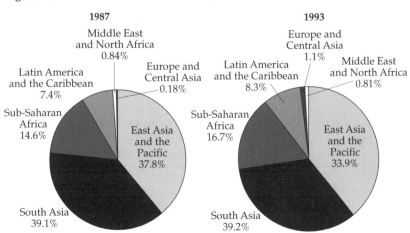

Source: Table 2.1 for East Asia and the Pacific; World Bank 1996c for other regions.

in China. In absolute terms the number of poor was more than halved in China and fell by almost three-quarters in Indonesia. As a result, by 1995 the two countries accounted for 84 percent of the region's poor. And although Indonesia's record is remarkable (the head-count index declined from 64.3 percent in 1975 to 11.4 percent in 1995), it was not the country with the largest proportional reduction between 1975 and 1995: Malaysia's was 95 percent (from 17.4 percent to less than 1 percent) and Thailand's was 90 percent (from 8.1 percent to less than 1 percent).

Because of China's size, changes in poverty there have a much larger impact on regional trends than in any other country. China still contains more than three-quarters of all the poor people in East Asia. It is of great interest, therefore, that the slowdown in Chinese poverty reduction after 1985, which was linked to growing inequality and slower rural income growth, seems to have been a transitory phenomenon (World Bank 1997b). The most recent data suggest a rapid recovery in poverty reduction since 1993, brought about largely by growth in rural incomes. Whereas the number of China's poor fell by less than 12 percent between 1985 and 1993, 1994–95 saw a reduction of almost 24 percent (box 2.2).

Naturally, the decline in the share of the region's poor living in China or Indonesia is offset by increases elsewhere. The countries where poverty reduction was slower than average and that account for a larger share of the poor today than they did ten or twenty years ago are Lao PDR, Mongolia, Papua New Guinea, the Philippines, and Vietnam, a trend driven largely by slower or delayed growth in these countries (figure 2.2). For example, the Philippines' share of the region's poor has more than doubled, from 2.1 percent in 1975 to 5.1 percent in 1995.

The combined share of Lao PDR, Mongolia, and Vietnam rose from 9.2 percent in 1985 to 10.2 percent in 1995.[4] The importance of this group in the region's poverty map is reinforced if we adopt another concept of poverty profile and focus on country head-counts rather than on proportion of the region's poor.[5] Lao PDR, Mongolia, and Vietnam are clearly a group apart in the head-count columns of table 2.1. In 1995 these three countries were the only ones with more than 40 percent of their population below the poverty line. Depth of poverty also sets them apart; their poverty gaps are substantially higher than those of any other economy in the region. Even if, as noted before, we need to be cautious about estimates of purchasing power parity exchange rates, the fact remains that extreme poverty is still widespread—the rule rather than the exception—across Indochina and Mongolia, but not so in the rest of East Asia, including China.

Box 2.2 Poverty Reduction in China: What Is behind the Stop-Go Pattern?

Four distinct phases are discernible in poverty and inequality trends in post-reform China. The first phase, 1978–84, was characterized by rapid growth in per capita incomes, reduced income inequality and rapid poverty reduction (see figure). The economy continued to grow during the second phase, 1984–91, but trends in income inequality were reversed and poverty incidence stagnated. The third phase, 1991–93, saw an acceleration of per capita income growth and the resumption of poverty reduction but a further widening of the income gap. Growth momentum continued during the fourth phase, 1993–95, when the rate of poverty reduction accelerated and income inequality declined.[1]

What explains this stop-go pattern? Because most poor people in China continue to rely on farming as the primary source of income, the environment for farming is a major part of the story. The three main components of agricultural reform that started in 1978 were abandoning collective farming, increasing prices for farm outputs, and relaxing quota restrictions and easing restrictions on inter-regional trade.

The combined result of these reforms was a growth in crop output from 2.6 percent a year during 1970–78 to 6.0 percent a year during 1978–84, expansion of the area under cash crops from 9.6 percent of total cropped area in 1978 to 13.5 percent in 1984, growth in the index of farm labor, which had remained constant during 1970–78, to 1.8 percent a year, and accelerated accumulation of farm capital, from 6.8 percent a year during 1970–78 to 8.7 percent a year during 1978–84.[2] The net impact was an average annual growth of 14 percent in rural per capita incomes and a proportional decline in poverty incidence of more than 25 percent.

The productivity effects faded by 1984, by which time all collectives had been dismantled. That, combined with increased government intervention in agricultural markets, resulted in a decline in the growth of crop output. During 1985–90 net rural per capita incomes grew by less than 3 percent a year and there was a significant slowdown in poverty reduction.

In the early 1990s the central government allowed provincial governments more flexibility in planning production levels and purchasing grain at fixed prices from farmers. This grain was then distributed to urban

(Box continues on next page.)

Box Figure Poverty and Inequality in China, 1981–95

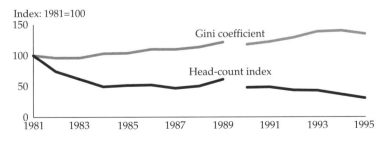

Box 2.2 (continued)

consumers at a low price through ration coupons, and farmers were given subsidized inputs. This improved the terms of trade for farm products and increased peasants' real income. By late 1993 most provincial governments had stopped supplying low-priced grain to urban residents, while many continued to use the quota system linking purchase to the provision of subsidized inputs. This led to a rapid rise in grain and edible oil prices. In early 1994 the central government reinstituted the quota system for specific grains and oilseeds but increased state-fixed prices. The result was a net improvement in rural income and rapid decline in the number of poor.

It is clear that there were two prominent sources of growth in farm incomes—improved prices for farm products (the pure terms of trade effect) and increased agricultural output per unit of land (the productivity effect). During 1978–84 both effects contributed to growth in farm incomes. Since 1984, however, poverty trends seem to be dictated mainly by changes in the terms of trade. Growth in agricultural yields since the mid-1980s has continued to decline, and during 1984–92 the share of individual investment in fixed assets of production in total investment in rural China declined dramatically.

Experience from other countries shows that agricultural productivity increases are closely linked to poverty reduction. Abolition of collective agriculture in China led to a one-off increase in productivity. To sustain productivity growth, however, a number of policy actions appear necessary, including further reform of grain markets, institutional changes in fertilizer marketing, investment in agricultural research and extension, and irrigation (World Bank 1997a). An issue of particular complexity and importance for the incomes and security of the poor is land policy. Several studies have pointed to weak property rights as one reason for the slowdown of growth in the farm sector. The household responsibility system individualized the claim to residual income while continuing to vest land ownership in the collective, thus discouraging farmers from making long term-investments in land (Wen 1995; Choe 1996). Some observers believe that granting absolute individual land rights will boost agricultural productivity and accelerate poverty reduction (Prosterman, Hanstad, and Ping 1996; Crook 1994). Other studies have also found at least preliminary empirical support for the hypothesis that land tenure insecurity is adversely affecting medium- and long-term investments on farms in China (Yao 1995; Feder and others 1992).[3] Others argue that the prevailing distribution of agricultural land is optimal for both equity and efficiency and that any policy change that could lead to land redistribution would result in equity and efficiency losses (Burgess 1997). Even if absolute individualization of land rights did not entail a loss in efficiency, whether it will actually lead to significant efficiency gains in the face of imperfect credit markets and other policy distortions in input and output markets remains to be investigated. At the very least, this debate suggests that a careful rethinking of China's policy toward agricultural land, with the objective of balancing productivity and income security objectives, is desirable.

Figure 2.2 Compostion of Poverty across East Asia, 1985 and 1995

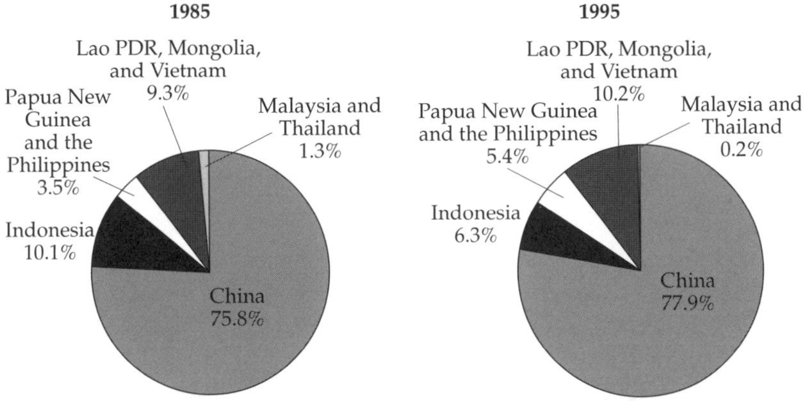

Source: Table 2.1.

General welfare improvements across the region are broadly confirmed by considering nonmonetary welfare indicators (table 2.2).
During 1973–90 the region saw substantial increases in life
expectancy at birth and declines in infant mortality. Similarly, access
to education expanded, with China and Indonesia reportedly joining
Korea and the Philippines in achieving universal primary net enrollment. In all four countries, as well as in Malaysia, secondary net
enrollment also expanded beyond 50 percent of children in the eligi-
ble age group.

Cross-country disparities are evident in these indicators, however.
While in 1993 around 1 in every 100 Malaysian or Korean live births led
to death in the first year of the child's life, in Lao PDR the rate was
almost 10 in every 100. Life expectancy was twenty years shorter there
than in Korea, Malaysia, or Taiwan (China), and eighteen years shorter
than in China. Lao PDR and Papua New Guinea also lagged behind in
terms of primary net enrollment, and even more so in secondary net
enrollment. Though differences in these indicators may be less marked
than income disparities, they are still significant. Those economies with
the highest poverty indices in East Asia—Mongolia and the countries
in Indochina—are also the ones with the lowest nonmonetary welfare
indicators.

It is not only across economies that poverty concentrations vary.
Within each economy there is pronounced variation in income across
geographical regions, education levels, and occupational groups. To
better understand the face of poverty within each country, we now turn
to national poverty profiles across various groups.

Table 2.2 Social Indicators in East Asia, 1970–95

Economy	Life expectancy at birth (years)		Infant mortality (per 1,000 live births)		Primary net enrollment (percent)		Secondary net enrollment (percent)	
	1970	1993	1970	1993	1970	1995	1970	1995
East Asia	59	68	76	34	n.a.	n.a.	n.a.	n.a.
Taiwan, China	69	75	n.a.	7	n.a.	>99	75	87
Korea, Rep. of	61	71	46	11	>99	>99	45	93
Malaysia	62	71	45	13	84	89	26	56
Thailand	58	69	73	36	79	88	18	35
Indonesia	48	63	118	56	76	>99	13	55
China	62	69	69	31	76	>99	35	51
Philippines	57	67	71	42	>99	>99	40	76
Papua New Guinea	47	56	112	67	31	70	4	13
Lao PDR	40	51	146	95	n.a.	60	n.a.	15[a]
Vietnam	49	65	111	41	n.a.	91	n.a.	45[a]
Mongolia	53	64	102	58	n.a.	n.a.	n.a.	n.a.

n.a. Not available.
a. Lower secondary.
Source: Ahuja and Filmer 1996; DGB, various years; World Bank 1995a and 1996e; World Bank data.

Profile of Poverty in East Asia

Recent World Bank poverty assessments and other sources help paint a picture of who the poor are in various East Asian economies. For each economy we use data from a single year, that of the most recent survey. Because the original studies from which these data are drawn focused on individual countries, poverty lines are country-specific. While this invalidates comparisons of absolute poverty levels across countries, broad trends in the composition of the poor are loosely comparable and suggestive. For all economies (except Malaysia and Thailand) per capita consumption expenditure is the measure of welfare. For Malaysia and Thailand the welfare measure is per capita income. Unless otherwise specified, estimates of the incidence of poverty measure the percentage of individuals in poverty (the head-count index).

In painting our picture of East Asian poverty, we consider the location (rural or urban, region), education, occupation, ethnicity, and gender of the household head. Wherever possible, we present both the group head-count—that is, the portion of the population in group k that is poor (H_k)—and the "poverty share" of each group—the portion of the poor population that belongs to the specific group k under consideration ($f_k H_k/H$) (see note 5).

Urban and Rural Poverty

Poverty in East Asia is still predominantly rural. This is true in every economy in the region for which we have estimates except Mongolia. The incidence and depth of poverty are substantially higher in rural areas (table 2.3). In Indonesia, Lao PDR, the Philippines, and Vietnam the incidence of poverty is twice as high in rural areas as in urban areas. In China and Malaysia the incidence of poverty in urban areas is particularly low. The chasm between urban and rural poverty is even wider if one considers the contribution of both groups to overall poverty. Because most of the East Asian population live in rural areas, which have higher head-counts, their contribution to the total number of poor far exceeds that from urban areas (table 2.4). For example, almost 90 percent of the poor in Lao PDR and Vietnam live in rural areas. Again, it is only in Mongolia that a larger share of the poor (57 percent) lives in urban areas.

Regional Poverty

There are substantial regional and provincial variations in standards of living—and therefore in the incidence of poverty—in most East Asian

Table 2.3 Poverty Estimates for Rural and Urban Households
(percent)

Country, year	Head-count index			Poverty gap index		
	Rural	Urban	Total	Rural	Urban	Total
Malaysia, 1987	24.7	7.3	18.6	n.a.	n.a.	n.a.
Thailand, 1992	15.5	2.4[a],16.8[b]	13.1	4.0	0.8[a],5.1[b]	3.5
Indonesia, 1990	23.6	10.7	19.6	4.3	1.7	3.5
China, 1995	31.0	0.8	22.2	9.5	0.2	7.0
Philippines, 1991	67.8	34.2	49.7	24.1	10.2	17.0
Papua New Guinea, 1996	39.4	13.5	35.4	12.8	3.4	11.3
Lao PDR, 1992/93	53.0	23.9	46.1	14.4	4.5	12.1
Vietnam, 1992/93	61.1	29.9	54.9	19.1	8.5	17.1
Mongolia, 1995	33.1	38.5	36.3	8.9	12.2	10.9

n.a. Not available.
Note: All estimates of poverty are based on country-specific poverty lines. For China the estimates are based on a poverty line of $1 a day.
a. Municipal (urban).
b. Sanitary (semiurban).
Source: World Bank data.

Table 2.4 Distribution of Poor in Rural and Urban Households
(percent)

Country, year	Rural	Urban	Total
Malaysia, 1987	86.0	14.0	100
Thailand, 1992	84.7	3.4[a],11.7[b]	100
Indonesia, 1990	83.4	16.6	100
China, 1995	98.9	1.1	100
Philippines, 1991	n.a.	n.a.	100
Papua New Guinea, 1996	94.2	5.8	100
Lao PDR, 1992/93	87.8	12.2	100
Vietnam, 1992/93	89.1	10.9	100
Mongolia, 1994/95	43.0	57.0	100

n.a. Not available.
Note: Poverty lines are country specific.
a. Municipal (urban).
b. Sanitary (semiurban).
Source: World Bank data.

economies (appendix figures B.1–B.7). The greatest regional variation in head-counts is found in the newly industrialized economies of Indonesia and Thailand, where aggregate poverty has fallen dramatically in the past twenty to thirty years, and in China. Aggregate reductions were not uniform across these economies, and the incidence of poverty remains high in some regions. For example, in 1990 poverty incidence in Indonesia ranged from 1.3 percent in Jakarta, to 18 percent in West Java, to a high of 46 percent in East Nusa Tenggara. However, the areas in Indonesia where poverty is highest are not the most populated. In terms of the distribution of the poor among provinces, it is the island of Java (central, eastern, and western Java) that houses most of the poor.[6] In Thailand, in contrast, the northeast has the highest incidence of poverty as well as the highest concentration of the poor, about 50 percent.

Even in countries such as Lao PDR and Vietnam, where poverty is still much more widespread, there are variations in poverty incidence in different parts of the country. In Vietnam the incidence of poverty ranges from a low of 33.7 percent in the southeast to 77.2 percent in the north-central region. As for the distribution of poor people, about 18 percent live in the north-central region, while less than 8 percent live in the southeast (appendix tables B.1–B.7).

Poverty and Education

Education is a strong correlate of poverty. In Vietnam households headed by individuals with no formal education are five times more likely to be poor than households headed by those with a university education (appendix figure B.12). This trend is also corroborated in Lao PDR, the Philippines, and Thailand, where we have similar tabulations. In the Philippines most of the poor (66 percent) live in households headed by someone with one to six years of schooling, and in Vietnam most of the poor live in households headed by someone with primary education (39 percent) or lower secondary education (35 percent; see appendix tables B.8–B.12 and appendix figures B.8–B.12).

The negative correlation between poverty and education is likely to reflect a two-way causal relationship, with lower education reducing earnings and increasing vulnerability to poverty, which in turn reduces a household's ability to educate its children. This mechanism is intrinsically intergenerational in nature: children living in poor households are in fact less likely to go to school. This can be documented in countries such as Indonesia, Lao PDR, Mongolia, and Vietnam, where data are collected on educational attainments and per capita expenditures for the same households (table 2.5).

In all four countries children living in poorer households have lower primary and substantially lower secondary enrollment ratios. In Vietnam, for example, the net enrollment rate at the primary level is 68 percent for the lowest expenditure quintile and 86 percent for the richest quintile. The difference in enrollment rates between rich and poor becomes even more pronounced at higher levels of education. In Vietnam, for instance, the net enrollment rate at the lower secondary level is 19 percent for the poorest quintile and 56 percent for the richest quintile; at the higher secondary level the corresponding numbers are 2 percent and 28 percent. In Indonesia the results are similar. At the primary level nearly universal enrollment implies that most of the poor have access. But at the lower secondary level the gap in net enrollment rates between the poorest decile and the richest decile increases more than eightfold (9 percent for the poorest decile and 76 percent for the richest decile). At the higher secondary level the gap widens to a thirty-fivefold difference.

Poverty and Occupation of Household Head

East Asian households headed by farmers face a higher incidence of poverty than households headed by people working in any other sector of the economy. This is evident in Indonesia, Lao PDR, the Philippines, Thailand, and Vietnam, countries for which poverty measures by occupation of household head are available (table 2.6 and appendix figures B.13–B.15). Not only is the incidence of poverty high in agriculture

Table 2.5 Distribution of Net Enrollment Rates
(percent)

Country, expenditure level (quintile)	Primary	Lower secondary	Higher secondary	Post-secondary
Indonesia, 1989[a]				
Poorest	82.0	8.8	1.9	0.0
Second	85.3	17.2	5.6	0.0
Third	88.4	22.0	7.7	0.1
Fourth	88.0	29.2	9.0	0.1
Fifth	91.0	34.7	16.1	0.4
Sixth	91.6	43.0	21.1	0.6
Seventh	92.0	48.3	27.2	1.3
Eighth	92.1	59.8	37.7	2.2
Ninth	94.4	66.4	49.4	5.0
Richest	94.4	75.9	69.1	26.9
Lao PDR, 1992/93				
Poorest	44.0	4.0	n.a.	n.a
Second	50.0	10.0	n.a.	n.a
Third	61.0	14.0	n.a.	n.a
Fourth	68.0	18.0	n.a.	n.a
Richest	78.0	28.0	n.a.	n.a
Vietnam, 1992/93				
Poorest	67.7	18.6	1.9	0.0
Second	77.3	25.7	3.0	0.4
Third	80.7	36.3	6.9	1.0
Fourth	84.7	44.2	12.8	1.9
Richest	86.2	56.0	27.6	7.0
Mongolia, 1995				
Poorest	74.0	64.0[b]		14.0
Second	84.0	80.0[b]		18.0
Third	80.0	77.0[b]		24.0
Fourth	84.0	80.0[b]		35.0
Richest	91.0	86.0[b]		40.0

n.a. Not available.
a. Data are based on income level, and are grouped by decile.
b. Secondary enrollment data are aggregated across lower and higher.
Source: World Bank data.

households, but the share of the poor who live in these households is also high: about 60 percent in the Philippines and 76 percent in Thailand and Vietnam. In Indonesia, too, the highest incidence of poverty is found among wage-earning farmers and self-employed farmers in rural areas. Since wage-earning and self-employed farmers together comprise about 43 percent of the population, this group accounts for 70 percent of the poor population (appendix tables B.13–B.17 and figures B.13–B.15).

Table 2.6 Poverty and Occupation or Sector of Employment of Household Head
(percent)

Country, year	Head-count index, agriculture	Head-count index, national	Share of agricultural households in total poor
Thailand, 1992	20.1	13.1	76.6
Indonesia, 1993	25.3[a]	12.6	13.6
	20.7[b]	n.a.	56.5
Philippines, 1991	70.7	49.7	60.3
Lao PDR, 1992/93	52.4	46.1	n.a.
Vietnam, 1992/93	64.5	54.9	75.9

n.a. Not available.
a. Rural laborer.
b. Rural self-employed.
Note: Poverty lines are country specific.
Source: World Bank data.

Poverty and Ethnicity

There is a growing view that the incidence of poverty may also vary significantly across ethnic groups within some economies in the region (see Sarvananthan 1997). While there is evidence of this for Malaysia and Vietnam, the data available at the national level are not sufficient to test the hypothesis in most of the region's other economies. In Vietnam most of the population (85 percent) belongs to the Kinh ethnic group (table 2.7). The incidence of poverty among the Kinh is slightly less than the national average. Except for the Chinese, other ethnic groups, who live in remote rural areas, have a higher incidence of poverty than the national average. The Chinese live predominantly in the urban areas of the relatively better-off southern Vietnam, and have a substantially lower incidence of poverty.

Malaysia is an interesting case to study in this context (see World Bank 1991). In the late 1960s Malaysia experienced political instability

Table 2.7 Vietnam: Distribution of Poverty by Ethnic Group, 1992–93
(percent)

Ethnic group	Head-count index	Contribution to total	Share of population
Kinh	52.2	80.3	84.5
Chinese	13.7	0.6	2.4
Other	79.9	19.1	13.1
National	54.9	100.0	100.0

Source: Dollar and Glewwe forthcoming.

Table 2.8 Malaysia: Poverty and Race, 1973 and 1987

	1973			1987		
Indicator	Malay	Chinese	Indian	Malay	Chinese	Indian
Household income	260	531	431	861	1,405	1,121
Family size	5.3	5.7	5.6	4.8	4.8	5.2
Per capita household income	50	94	77	179	290	218
Head-count index (percent)	54.6	20.1	28.2	21.3	4.2	9.2

Source: World Bank 1991.

stemming in part from a high incidence of poverty and racial differences in living standards and opportunities. In response, the government introduced the New Economic Policy in the Second Malaysia Plan (1971–75), whose explicit objectives were to reduce poverty, improve living conditions by expanding primary education and health care, and eliminate racial differences in employment and asset ownership.

In 1973 the incidence of poverty (percentage of households in poverty) was highest among Malays (54.6 percent), followed by Indians (28 percent) and Chinese (20 percent; table 2.8). By 1987 the poverty incidence had declined for all three races: it was 21 percent for Malays, 9 percent for Indians, and 4 percent for Chinese. A regression analysis (logit model for the probability of being poor), that controls for sex, region of residence, dependency ratio, urban-rural location, educational attainment, and race shows that in 1973 a Chinese household had a 26 percentage point lower probability of being poor relative to a Malay household, and an Indian household a 16 percentage point lower prob-

Table 2.9 Malaysia: Age Cohorts with Post-Primary Schooling, 1957 and 1984
(percent)

	Males					
Age		1957			1984	
group	Malay	Chinese	Indian	Malay	Chinese	Indian
15–19	23	32	34	89	84	79
20–24	14	23	24	81	73	74
25–34	9	20	25	60	59	62
35–44	9	22	19	31	42	49
45–54	6	14	14	14	23	31
55–64	3	10	12	5	14	15
65+	2	8	11	4	10	9

n.a. Not available.
Note: Post-primary schooling means more than six years of education.
Source: World Bank 1991, p. 68.

ability. By 1987 this gap had fallen to 7 percentage points for Chinese and 3 percentage points for Indians (World Bank 1991). While these improvements reflect both the overall decline in poverty incidence and a reduction in the Chinese-Malay mean income gap, it is less clear that the Chinese-Indian mean income gap has been reduced.

The New Economic Policy resulted in improved education across the board (table 2.9). In 1957 Malays had substantially lower educational levels than Indians and Chinese. Even for the youngest age cohort of males (15–19 years), 32 percent of Chinese had post-primary education (more than six years of education), compared with 23 percent of Malays. For older age cohorts the differences were more pronounced. By 1984 this had changed dramatically. For the two youngest cohorts of males Malays had slightly higher percentages with post-primary education than Indians or Chinese. A similar picture arises for females, who have effectively caught up with males over the period. Both developments are less marked for older age cohorts, many of whom were educated before the New Economic Policy began.

Poverty and Gender

The gender-poverty connection can be examined from many angles. In terms of consumption poverty, the most commonly used yardstick (and perhaps the least satisfactory) is gender of the household head (table 2.10). In most countries for which such a tabulation is available, the incidence of poverty is higher for male-headed households, and the

Females						
	1957				1984	
Malay	Chinese	Indian		Malay	Chinese	Indian
8	17	14		88	81	n.a.
3	10	10		74	63	n.a.
1	7	9		44	45	n.a.
4	5	4		17	28	n.a.
–	2	3		3	9	n.a.
–	1	2		2	6	n.a.
–	–	2		–	2	n.a.

majority of the poor live in those households. Only in Mongolia and Papua New Guinea is the incidence of poverty significantly higher in female-headed households than in male-headed households. However, in Papua New Guinea only 6 percent of households are headed by females, so their contribution to total poverty is small.

But household headship is increasingly recognized as an unsatisfactory handle on any real differences that might exist between the standards of living of men and women (for examples from other countries, see Quisumbing and others 1995 and Ferreira and Litchfield 1996). Even though it is hard to measure individual poverty, and our understanding of intrahousehold resource allocation is far from complete, it is possible that poverty may exacerbate gender disparities. An examination of welfare outcomes by gender for both poor and non-poor households in a country is often suggestive. For example, in Lao PDR the net primary enrollment ratio for males among the poorest quintile is 51 percent; for females it is 37 percent (World Bank 1995a). In contrast, in the richest quintile the ratio goes up to 77 percent for males and 79 percent for females.

At least two other dimensions of inequality between men and women should be taken into consideration when assessing the difference in real welfare levels across gender: intrahousehold distributional issues and earnings differentials in the labor market.

Our understanding of intrahousehold allocation decisions is often limited by the lack of individually disaggregated consumption data. Deaton (1989) proposes a method using household-level expenditure data that allows him to make some inferences about the allocation of goods to different types of individuals within a household. The idea

Table 2.10 Poverty and Gender of Household Head
(percent)

Country, year	Male head		Female head		Female-headed households as share of total
	Head-count index	Contribution to total	Head-count index	Contribution to total	
Thailand, 1992	13.2	83.9	12.6	16.1	16.8
Philippines, 1991	51.8	92.3	33.2	7.7	11.3[a]
Papua New Guinea, 1996	34.7	91.6	46.2	8.4	6.4
Lao PDR, 1992/93	46.5	n.a.	38.6	n.a.	n.a.
Vietnam, 1992/93	57.2	80.7	46.9	19.3	22.5
Mongolia, 1994/95	31.5	70.9	58.4	29.2	18.4

n.a. Not available.
Note: Poverty lines are country specific.
a. Computed from group head-count indices and the national head-count index.
Source: World Bank data.

behind the test is that for households with the same level of income and occupation, those with children will spend less on "adult" goods than households with no children. Among households with children, the analysis tests if the reduction in adult-goods expenditure is larger for households with female children or for those with male children. For evidence of gender bias, the latter must be true systematically. This method was applied to Côte d'Ivoire and Thailand. The results confirm that the presence of additional children reduces expenditures on adult goods. For Côte d'Ivoire there is no evidence of bias in favor of boys. In rural Thailand there appears to be some such bias in intrahousehold resource allocation, but it is small and statistically insignificant (see Deaton 1997 for a review of the evidence on intrahousehold allocation and gender bias and Burgess and Zhuang 1996 for evidence on China).

While much has been written on gender wage gaps in industrial countries (see, for example, Oaxaca 1973 and Gunderson 1989), this is a relatively new strand of research for East Asia. Agrawal and Walton (1996) summarize evidence on the gender wage gap in the region, arguing that there is no systematic relationship between the level of economic development and (unconditional) female-male wage ratios. For the available sample of Asian countries that relationship is heavily influenced by historical and cultural factors, leading to low ratios in Japan and Korea and to a high ratio in China, where wage setting has been centrally planned (table 2.11). In 1990 the unconditional ratio of female to male earnings in the manufacturing sector ranged from a low of 50 percent for Japan to a high of 86 percent in China (Meng 1996). Also, within a given country relative wage differentials across genders do not necessarily narrow with economic development. The gender wage gap in manufacturing actually increased in Hong Kong (China), Japan, and Taiwan (China), improved in Korea and Singapore, and

Table 2.11 Female Earnings in Manufacturing, 1980s and 1990s
(percentage of male earnings)

Economy	1980s	1990s
Hong Kong, China	74	70
Japan	53	50
Singapore	62	71
Taiwan, China	66	61
Korea, Rep. of	46	54
Malaysia	73	n.a.
Thailand	70	n.a.
China	85	86
Philippines	62	n.a.

n.a. Not available.
Source: Meng 1996, taken from Agrawal and Walton 1996.

remained stable in China. Case studies of Hong Kong (China), Korea, and Taiwan (China) suggest that initial gaps in education and labor market experience can be narrowed by investments in women that equalize educational opportunities (Agrawal and Walton 1996). But perhaps because of labor market discrimination an unexplained wage gap persists that may be less responsive to policy and legislative measures, as the experience of industrial countries suggests.

The gender aspect of the region's poverty profile must be further explored, and future research should focus on issues that are more difficult, but also more relevant: labor market issues and intrahousehold resource allocation.

3
Inequality in East Asia:
Recent Trends

D espite high poverty levels in some East Asian countries, such as Lao PDR and Mongolia, and among certain groups in other countries—farmers in the Philippines, residents of north-east Thailand, non-Chinese ethnic minorities in Vietnam—the general picture presented in chapter 2 is unambiguously positive: poverty has been declining in every East Asian economy for which we have data except Papua New Guinea. And yet there is some apprehension in the region about East Asia's "growth with equity" experience. After three decades in which "rapid growth and reduced inequality [were] the defining characteristics of what has come to be known as the East Asian economic miracle" (World Bank 1993a, p. 27), there is growing evidence that inequality is beginning to rise in some of the region's economies.

It is not clear that inequality in East Asia was ever exceptionally low.[7] For a long time good household surveys, and hence reliable income distribution statistics, were scarce. The recent boom in such surveys has enabled researchers to compile much more comprehensive data sets on inequality measures across countries, the largest set being that described by Deininger and Squire (1996).[8] It is now possible to compare more countries in East Asia with more countries elsewhere, and to better compare regions of the world (table 3.1). Care should be taken in comparing the decades listed in table 3.1, however, since the composition of regions can change because the availability of surveys varies.

The data set in table 3.1 contains Gini coefficients based on both income distributions and expenditure distributions, which are not comparable. Since a country's income distribution is generally more unequal than its expenditure distribution, and since Latin America and Eastern Europe have a higher share of income Gini coefficients than other regions, their average inequality is overstated in the table. Nonetheless, Deininger and Squire's comparisons are a useful reflection of general orders of magnitude of inequality across regions. While East Asia is clearly more egalitarian than Latin America or Sub-Saharan Africa, it is by no means the most egalitarian region in the world. On average, the former socialist countries of Eastern Europe (even during their transition in the 1990s), the high-income countries, and South Asia

Table 3.1 Inequality in Various Regions, 1980s and 1990s
(averaged Gini coefficients)

Region	1980s	1990s
Eastern Europe	25.01	28.94
High-income countries	33.23	33.75
South Asia	35.01	31.88
East Asia and the Pacific	38.70	38.09
Middle East and North Africa	40.45	38.03
Sub-Saharan Africa	43.46	46.95
Latin America and the Caribbean	49.75	49.31

Note: The total sample includes 108 economies. Although Gini coefficients come from household surveys that satisfy comprehensiveness criteria in terms of both geographical coverage and income sources, they nevertheless include unadjusted data from both expenditure and income distributions. The proportion of income Gini coefficients varies across regions, hampering comparability. Regional averages are unweighted, and changes across the two decades may be due to changes in the composition of the sample. The numbers merely suggest broad orders of magnitude.
Source: Deininger and Squire 1996.

are more equal. Countries in the Middle East and North Africa have the same broad range of inequality as East Asia.

More important, some recent surveys suggest that inequality is rising in some countries (table 3.2).[9] It has clearly risen in China, Hong Kong (China), and Thailand. It also appears to have inched up in Korea and the Philippines, although the changes in these cases would fall within the margins of error of the estimated Ginis. The same is true of the small declines in Indonesia and Singapore. The only country showing a pronounced decline in inequality was Malaysia, from 1973 to 1989. Although lack of historical data precludes empirical conclusions about inequality trends in Mongolia and Indochina, there, as in China, the dynamics of economic reform may well be putting upward pressure on inequality.

What lies behind East Asia's incipient, and clearly not universal, rise in inequality? While a systematic causal analysis lies beyond the scope of this study, certain decompositions of inequality in Thailand suggest that there may be two basic mechanisms at play: an increase in the returns to higher levels of education, driving a wedge between highly skilled workers and those with primary or lower secondary education; and a growing spatial disparity in economic prosperity, stemming from a concentration of economic activity (in value-added terms) in certain areas, to the exclusion of others.

The first of these trends may be of greater importance to richer economies in the region, including Hong Kong (China), Taiwan (China), and Thailand. In these cases economic growth has entailed a

Table 3.2 Inequality in East Asia

		Gini coefficient	
Economy, period	Measured variable	First year	Last year
Hong Kong, China, 1971–91	Income per household	40.9	45.0
Singapore, 1973–89	Income per household	41.0	39.0
Taiwan, China, 1985–95	Income per household	29.0	31.7
Korea, Rep. of, 1970–88	Income per household	33.3	33.6
Malaysia, 1973–89	Income per capita	50.1	45.9
Thailand, 1975–92[a]	Expenditure per capita	36.4	46.2
Indonesia, 1970–95	Expenditure per capita	34.9	34.2
China, 1985–95 (total)[b]	Income per capita	29.9	38.8
China, 1985–95 (urban)[b]	Income per capita	19.0	27.5
China, 1985–95 (rural)[b]	Income per capita	27.1	33.9
Philippines, 1985–94	Expenditure per capita	41.0	42.9
Papua New Guinea, 1996	Expenditure per capita	50.9	
Lao PDR, 1993	Expenditure per capita	30.4	
Vietnam, 1993	Expenditure per capita	35.4	
Mongolia, 1995	Expenditure per capita	33.2	

Note: The data in this table may be marginally different than those reported in other World Bank reports based on unit-record data. For the sake of consistency across countries we only report Ginis based on grouped data, except for Korea, Hong Kong (China), and Singapore, which are from Deininger and Squire 1996, and Taiwan (China), which are from DGB 1996.

a. Thailand is the only country for which we can present Ginis based on both expenditure and income distributions. The income per capita–based Gini was 42.6 percent in 1975 and 54.6 percent in 1992.

b. Because of China's size as well as with valuing home production of grain for own consumption, controlling for spatial price variations, and valuing in-kind transfers, the uncertainty associated with Chinese Ginis may be even greater than that for other economies (see World Bank 1997b for a detailed discussion).

Source: Deininger and Squire 1996; DGB 1996; World Bank staff estimates.

shifting structure of comparative advantage, with the composition of output gradually reflecting a movement up the "product ladder," in the direction of increasing the technology intensity of products. Because technology and skilled labor are generally complements in production, this shift has increased the demand for skilled labor, as well as the level of skills demanded. Given the emphasis most governments in the region placed on education, the supply of skilled labor also rose, providing the human resources to fuel growth while preventing a substantial stretching of the wage distribution. Recently, however, the rate of increase in the demand for skills seems to have outstripped the rate of increase in their supply in these economies. While these successful economies seem able to find niches in ever more technologically intensive sectors, the education production function does seem to run into decreasing returns to scale. Success in increasing access to primary (and in some cases secondary) education has enlarged the pool of workers with an intermediate range of skills, holding their wages down relative to those at the upper end of the skill distribution, whose incomes have soared.

In addition, in some cases migration from poorer countries has swelled the ranks of unskilled labor. This may have dampened the rise in wages at the lower end of the distribution that might have been expected with greater access to basic education. And there is concern in Hong Kong (China), Korea, Malaysia, Singapore, and Taiwan (China) that, where immigration does not prevent a rise in the wages of the unskilled workers, exporting the industries that demand unskilled labor (through foreign direct investment) will have the same effect. There is some evidence for these trends, though they are so recent and the evidence sufficiently anecdotal that further research is needed to corroborate them.

There is perhaps more evidence for the second trend, particularly in China, where growth rates differ significantly across provinces and between rural and urban areas. While substantial growth in agricultural incomes over the past two years serves as a warning against oversimplification, the fact remains that rural-urban and interprovincial income disparities in China have increased over the past fifteen years (box 3.1).[10] Spatial inequality has translated into interpersonal inequality, and this has been exacerbated by the biases of an urban welfare system that favors those who work for state enterprises and other government agencies. As a result Chinese migrants find it difficult to gain access to health, education, and housing facilities, which raises the net costs of migration (World Bank 1997a). The policy issues arising from this are important and complex, as they involve tradeoffs between the potential benefits of relaxing restrictions on labor mobility and the possible costs associated with a large inflow of poor migrants into China's already crowded cities.

One further question should be addressed with respect to inequality in East Asia. The evidence suggests that income distributions are no longer as stable in the region as they may once have been. Income inequality or expenditure inequality—or both—are rising in some countries. Does this matter? Given that economic growth continues apace and poverty reduction seems to be accelerating, should increases in inequality be of any concern to policymakers?

There are three basic reasons inequality may be regarded as undesirable. The first is that, for a given growth rate, an increase in inequality will tend to lead to less poverty reduction than if it had not occurred, through a reduction in the growth elasticity of poverty.[11] Datt and

Box 3.1 Why Is China Becoming More Unequal?

The rural-urban gap and interprovincial inequality have contributed most to the rise in inequality in China. A decomposition analysis presented in a recent World Bank report suggests that during 1985–95 the widening gap between rural and urban incomes was the main reason for this rise (see figure). The next most important reason was the interprovincial gap. The relative contributions of intrarural and intraurban inequality, though large, declined over the past decade.

The two-stage decomposition was carried out by partitioning the population first into rural and urban areas. The rural-urban inequality component is the between-group element of that decomposition. The remaining within-group Theils—one for rural areas and one for urban areas—were then decomposed by province. The sum of the between-group components for both second-stage decompositions was the interprovincial element. The within-group components for the rural and urban Theils were labeled intrarural and intraurban inequality, respectively.

It is inherent in this methodology that decompositions by individual attributes do not control for one another, and that in doing two-stage decompositions, the order of choice of partition matters for the outcome (see appendix A). Had the two-stage decomposition proceeded in the reverse order (by provinces first and then by urban-rural), the resulting bars would have been different heights. A suitable methodology for deriving a conceptually acceptable average of these two approaches has not yet been developed. Since the main finding—that rural-urban inequality appears to have increased by more and to be more important than the interprovincial component—is robust across the two orderings, we present this figure as an illustration. The reader should understand it as the outcome of the specific method just described, and not as a unique decomposition by both attributes.

Box Figure Components of China's Rising Inequality, 1985 and 1995

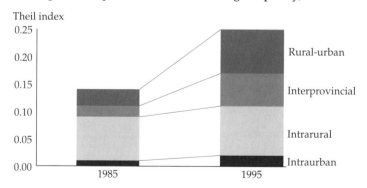

Source: World Bank 1997b.

Ravallion (1992) look at this from another angle, decomposing changes in poverty into effects due to growth and those due to distributional change (see chapter 5).

The second reason is that individuals in a society may place intrinsic value on equality and the sense of social cohesion arising from it. There is a long, distinguished line of proponents of this view. Plato argued that no one should be more than four times richer than the poorest member of society, so as to minimize the risk of the "greatest social evil," civil war (see Atkinson and Stiglitz 1980, p. 404). The Utilitarians proposed formulations of social welfare that placed a positive weight on increases in any person's income level, but with the weights declining with initial income. Their formulations, typified by Paretian social welfare functions, imply that mean-preserving equalizing transfers increase overall social welfare.[12] Today in East Asia the dislike of extreme income differences is being manifested in two ways: doubts about the fairness of the process by which the new super-rich have amassed their wealth, and a general aversion to displays of extreme wealth. Though hard evidence can only come from opinion surveys, which are beyond the scope of this study, there appears to be anecdotal evidence for both concerns.

Those who argue that it is equal opportunities rather than equal outcomes that characterize a just society will generally agree that extreme income inequality presents insurmountable obstacles to equality of opportunity. For complex societies it is hard to think of any better measure of the "distribution of opportunity" than the distribution of income, although in predominantly rural settings a case might be made for focusing on land distribution. A number of recent studies suggest ways in which income inequality is directly related to the distribution of opportunity, through credit markets or through access to political influence or education (see below). There is some historical and cultural evidence that East Asian societies may place an even greater value on social cohesion, including equality, than many other societies. The concern with which recent increases in inequality have been greeted in countries such as Thailand is suggestive.

The third reason to view inequality as undesirable is that, all other things being equal, it may hamper economic growth. The relationship between inequality and growth has become a popular topic for theoretical and empirical economists alike, and there is an unresolved debate as to how important the link is. While it is broadly agreed that growth does not lead systematically to greater income dispersion, there is some disagreement as to whether inequality hampers growth. On the basis of a simple statistical analysis of their international inequality database, Deininger and Squire (1996) suggest that no systematic link exists between initial income inequality and subsequent growth rates (though they do find evidence that unequal land distribution leads to slower growth).

Others have suggested that greater initial inequality is likely to reduce an economy's growth rate. Some analysts have focused on the consequences of imperfect capital markets, which can lead to credit constraints on agents (generally, but not always, the poor) and hence to lower productivity and efficiency losses (Aghion and Bolton 1997; Banerjee and Newman 1991 and 1993; Ferreira 1995; Galor and Zeira 1993). Others have suggested a political economy channel: greater inequality increases the support of the median voter for inefficient redistributive policies, and hence encourages efficiency losses and lower growth. This is the argument in models by Persson and Tabellini (1994) and Alesina and Rodrik (1994), who also offer empirical analyses associating higher initial inequality with lower growth.[13] On balance, it seems that there are plausible reasons why a very unequal distribution of incomes (or of wealth) will not help future aggregate economic growth. While it is likely that this relationship does not hold monotonically for all levels of inequality, it does help explain why increases in inequality—particularly if they are as rapid as those observed in China and Thailand—are unwelcome.

4
A Case Study of Thailand, 1975–92

To gain more insight into the evolution of inequality under rapid growth, it is helpful to focus on one country, Thailand. (Examples of other studies focusing on Thailand include Jitsuchon 1990; Kakwani and Krongkaew 1996 and 1997a; Meesook 1979; Rueda-Sabater and associates 1985.) The fact that Thailand experienced an increasing incidence of poverty during 1975–85 and then a rapidly declining incidence during 1985–95, as well as significant distributional shifts during the past two decades, makes it a suitable candidate for a case study. Thailand's experience is not representative of that of other economies in the region. The case of Thailand merely allows us to investigate the evolutionary phenomenon in greater detail, with access to household-level data. We first examine how the profile of the poor changed during 1975–92, then turn to the evolution of inequality and its determinants.

The data used in the analysis are from socioeconomic surveys conducted by Thailand's National Statistical Office. Detailed analysis is presented for two years: 1975 and 1992, but when discussing overall trends we also present estimates for two intervening years, 1981 and 1986. The surveys collect detailed information on household incomes and expenditures, housing characteristics, and the ownership of durables, using a two-stage sampling technique, and give representative national and regional estimates for the population when appropriate sample weights are used.

The welfare indicator, real household expenditures per capita, is comprehensive, including food and beverages, clothing, footwear, education, and other nonfood expenditures. The 1975 and 1992 household surveys, though largely comparable, differ in one potentially significant respect. The surveys have been administered every two years since 1986. To contain costs, a short-form food consumption module was administered first in the 1988 survey, and thereafter every four years. Thus the 1992 survey is based on the short questionnaire, which asks about for the consumption of 15 to 20 major food categories in a typical week, in contrast to the long one, which covers the consumption of about 140 food items on a daily basis for a week. The bias introduced by comparing expenditures based on the long questionnaire (in 1975) and the short questionnaire (in 1992) is an empirical issue. (A summary of the cross-country experience on the level of disaggregation of consumption items and its implications for the measurement of total consumption is summarized in Deaton and Grosh 1997.)[14] While detailed assessment of potential biases in measurement is beyond the scope of this study, initial analysis suggests that such biases would not call into question our major findings. An extension of the analysis using more recent survey data is planned.

All expenditures are expressed in 1992 Bangkok prices using the 1992 spatial price index reported by Kakwani and Krongkaew (1996) and regional consumer price indices. There has been a lively debate about where to draw the poverty line in Thailand (see Kakwani and Krongkaew 1996). We have chosen an international poverty line, $2 a day, for the analysis of changes in the poverty profile, though aggregate estimates based on a $1 a day poverty line are also presented to allow comparison with estimates presented in other sections of this study.

Based on the $2 a day poverty line, the incidence of poverty in Thailand declined dramatically between 1975 and 1981, from 42 percent to 30 percent (table 4.1). The next five years, however, saw an increase in the share of population falling below the poverty line, a trend consistent with that reported in Krongkaew, Tinakorn, and Suphachalasai (1996). The increase in poverty during 1981–86 is partly attributed to the significant drop in agricultural prices in 1986, which adversely affected agricultural households. However, poverty incidence continued to decline, albeit marginally, in urban areas over the same period. Since 1986 there has been a steady decline in poverty incidence. The depth and severity of poverty mirror the trend in the head-count index.

Changes in the Poverty Profile

This section examines the changes in the profile of poverty over 1975–92. The profiles are constructed along the following dimensions: region;

Table 4.1 Thailand: Measures of Poverty, 1975–92

Poverty line/measure	1975	1981	1986	1992
Poverty line: $2 a day (1985 prices)				
P(0) Head-count	41.80	30.36	33.80	15.69
P(1) Poverty gap	12.09	7.87	10.05	3.45
P(2) Poverty severity	4.79	2.87	4.15	1.14
Poverty line: $1 a day (1985 prices)				
P(0) Head-count	5.92	2.84	5.49	0.97
P(1) Poverty gap	0.94	0.39	1.08	0.16
P(2) Poverty severity	0.25	0.09	0.34	0.04

Source: Authors' calculations from Socioeconomic Survey data.

urban/rural status; education, sex, and occupation of the household head; and socioeconomic status of the household. In 1975 the incidence of poverty in rural areas was 51 percent (figure 4.1; appendix table C.1). This was twice the rate in semiurban areas and five times the rate in urban areas. Because 73 percent of the Thai population during that time lived in rural areas, the proportion of the poor living in rural areas was even higher, 89 percent. Rural areas continued to register the highest incidence of poverty in 1992. Despite the fact that the share of population in rural areas declined slightly, poverty was increasingly concentrated in these areas. In 1992 the proportion of the poor living in rural areas had increased to 94 percent. Poverty in urban areas declined sharply during 1975–92, from about 10 percent to just 1 percent.

Regional rankings of poverty have remained stable over time (figure 4.2). The northeast has the highest incidence, followed by the north, south, and central regions, and Bangkok and its vicinity. The population shares of each region have remained largely unchanged. However, there has been an increase in the concentration of the poor, with the share of the poor living in the northeast increasing from 50 percent in 1975 to 59 percent in 1992. A closer look at the breakdown by region shows that the increase in the concentration of the poor is entirely due to the rises in the share of the rural northeast.

The surveys also classify households by socioeconomic group (appendix table C.2). In general, households were classified by the principal source of livelihood and the employment status of the primary income earner, usually the household head.

Figure 4.1 Thailand: Incidence of Poverty by Location of Residence, 1975 and 1992

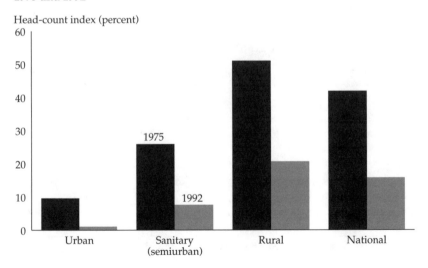

Head-count index (percent)

Farm operators, both owners and renters of land, faced the highest risk of poverty in 1975 (figure 4.3). Except for large farm operators, other households in this socioeconomic group faced high and similar risks of poverty. Farm workers and general workers also had a higher incidence of poverty than the national average. The poverty incidence of households classified as professional, clerical, sales, and service workers was among the lowest. By 1992 farm workers had the highest incidence of poverty, followed by landowners with between 2 and 40 rais of land. While the proportion of the population living in households classified as farm operators-owners declined significantly over this period, their share among the poor was almost unchanged. The share of farm workers among the poor more than doubled, going from 6 to 14 percent, while their share in the population increased from a little less than 5 percent to 6 percent. Households classified as professional, clerical, sales, and service workers continued to face a low risk of poverty. In 1992 this group comprised 27 percent of the total population but accounted for less than 10 percent of the poor.

Economically inactive households that primarily received assistance, pensions, or property income had a lower incidence of poverty than the national average in both years, and their share among the poor increased marginally less than their share in the total population.

The inverse correlation between the education of the household head and poverty incidence has been a consistent finding in all East Asian economies for which we have data. The evidence for Thailand corroborates this finding (appendix table C.3). In 1975 the incidence of poverty was highest for households in which the head had no formal education or

Figure 4.2 Thailand: Incidence of Poverty by Region, 1975 and 1992

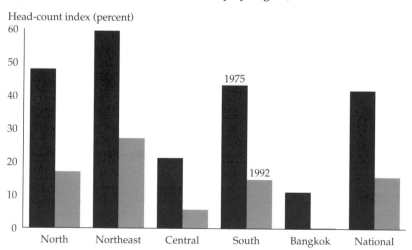

Head-count index (percent)

Figure 4.3 Thailand: Incidence of Poverty by Socioeconomic Class of Household, 1975 and 1992

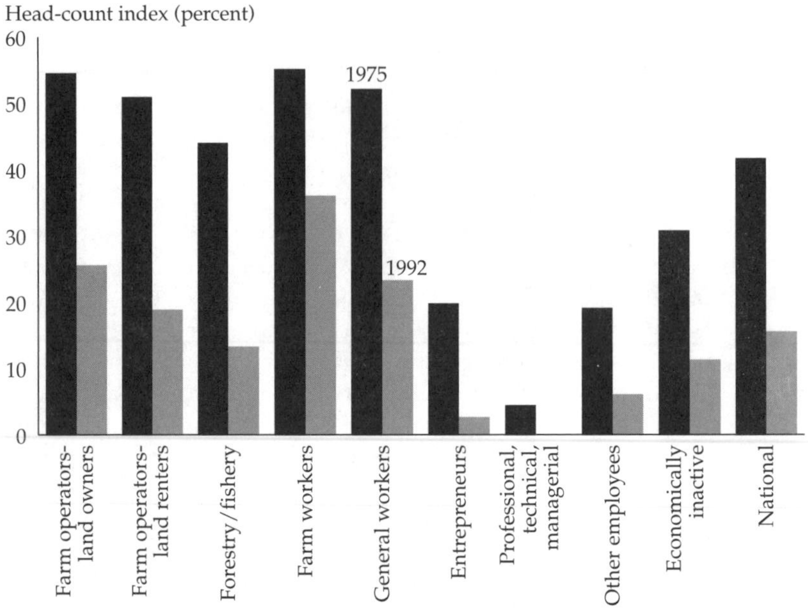

Head-count index (percent)

one to four years of elementary schooling (figure 4.4). Most of the population (67 percent) lived in households headed by people with one to four years of elementary schooling, and this group constituted about 72 percent of the poor. Another quarter of the poor lived in households headed by individuals with no education. During 1975–92 all groups registered substantial declines in poverty head-counts, but the proportional decline was smallest in the group of households headed by individuals with no education—38 percent, compared with more than 60 percent for households whose heads had lower elementary to upper secondary education.

By 1992, with the expansion in education, the proportion of the Thai population living in households headed by an uneducated person had declined to 11 percent, a drop of more than 50 percent. But the percentage of this group that was poor was almost twice that, 20 percent. Uneducated households had the highest incidence of poverty (29 percent), followed by households headed by persons with one to four years of schooling. In short, over the eighteen-year period poverty became more concentrated among those with no education and stayed concentrated among those with just a few years of schooling. Female-headed households continued to face a relatively lower risk of poverty, and there were no noticeable differences in the rate of poverty reduction between male- and female- headed households (see appendix table C.3).

Figure 4.4 Thailand: Incidence of Poverty by Education of Household Head, 1975 and 1992

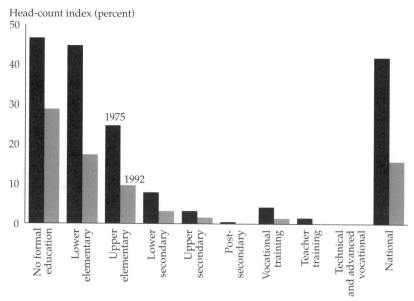

Head-count index (percent)

To summarize the patterns, the incidence of poverty remained relatively stable. Rural areas, the northeast, less-educated household heads, and agricultural workers faced the highest risk of poverty in 1975 and continued to do so in 1992. As total poverty declined over time, it became increasingly concentrated in rural areas, the rural northeast, uneducated households, and more generally households that depended on agriculture for their livelihood.

Changes in Inequality and Its Determinants

The vectors of expenditure used in constructing measures of inequality are identical to the ones used in creating poverty profiles. Table 4.2 presents the Gini coefficient as well as three additional indices, all of which belong to the generalized entropy class of inequality measures: $E(0)$ is the mean log deviation, $E(1)$ is the Theil index, and $E(2)$ is half of the square of the coefficient of variation. While all scalar inequality measures are essentially aggregates of distances between expenditures (or incomes), or between expenditures and the "center" of a distribution, different indices are constructed to be sensitive to different ranges of the distribution. In particular, while the mean log deviation is especially sensitive to incomes at the bottom of the distribution, and the Gini coef-

Table 4.2 Thailand: Expenditure Distribution and Inequality, 1975–92

Measure	1975	1981	1986	1992
Mean expenditures (baht)	947.5	1,250.0	1,261.3	1,911.4
Gini coefficient	35.74	39.71	42.62	45.39
E(0)	0.209	0.259	0.301	0.342
E(1)	0.245	0.305	0.335	0.406
E(2)	0.497	0.653	0.550	0.801

Note: All expenditures are in 1992 Bangkok prices.
Source: Authors' calculations from Socioeconomic Survey data.

ficient to those around the center, E(2) is more sensitive to higher incomes. The Theil index is constructed for constant responsiveness across all income ranges. Appendix A presents the formulas behind these indices and discusses some of their properties. (For further discussion of the generalized entropy class of inequality measures, see Cowell 1995.)

Inequality has been rising rapidly in Thailand. All the measures listed in table 4.2 show a steady increase since 1975 (except for E(2), which declines between 1981 and 1986, then increases sharply in 1992). In addition to being monotonic for three out of four measures, the rise is remarkable for its magnitude. Though these figures come from disaggregated and adjusted household-level data, the rise in the Gini coefficient is close to that presented in table 3.2. Its magnitude is now confirmed by substantial increases in three other measures, and there can be little doubt that the past two decades have seen a real increase in the dispersion of the Thai income distribution.[15]

An alternative—and more robust—way to describe the evolution of inequality over time in a country is through stochastic dominance analysis. In a nutshell, this type of analysis allows us to reach conclusions about changes in inequality and social welfare that are robust to the inequality (or welfare) index chosen, within fairly broad categories. (See Cowell 1995 and the references therein for a discussion and the proofs of the theorems of stochastic dominance.)

The concept relevant for inequality comparisons is Lorenz dominance (or mean-normalized second-order stochastic dominance). If the Lorenz curve for distribution A lies nowhere below and somewhere above that for distribution B, it is said that distribution A Lorenz dominates distribution B. In that case, a theorem attributed to Atkinson (1970) establishes that inequality is lower in distribution A than in distribution B for any inequality measure that satisfies the Pigou-Dalton transfer axiom.[16] In the case of Thailand, an analysis of Lorenz dominances over time provides robust confirmation of the trend of increasing inequality. As table 4.3 indicates, all four Lorenz dominances are of

Table 4.3 Thailand: Stochastic Dominance Analysis Results, 1975–92

	1975	1981	1986	1992
1975		LD	LD	LD
1981	FSD			LD
1986				
1992	FSD	FSD	FSD	

Note: FSD is first-order stochastic dominance; LD is Lorenz dominance. An entry in cell (i, j) indicates dominance of that type by year i over year j. Each of these dominance results is for the entire disaggregated sample and is significant at the 10 percent level for at least 99 percent of the range of distribution. The inference test was the intersection-union dominance statistical test (Howes 1993), based on the mean-difference test.

earlier years over later years (that is, above the diagonal). In particular, 1975 had a more equal distribution of expenditure than any subsequent year in the sample, and 1981 dominates 1992. The Lorenz criterion does not permit an unambiguous ranking of 1981 and 1986, as could have been inferred by the behavior of $E(2)$ in table 4.2, or of 1986 and 1992.

The Lorenz curves on which these statistically significant dominance results are based are shown in figure 4.5. But inequality is not the only concept that can benefit from the robustness of stochastic dominance analysis; first-order stochastic dominance can generate strong results

Figure 4.5 Thailand: Real Expenditure Lorenz Curves, 1975–92

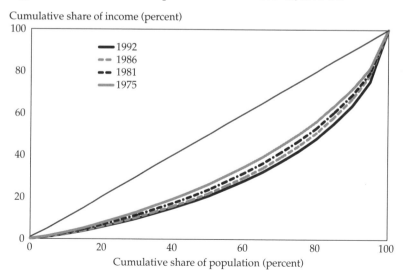

Figure 4.6 Thailand: Cumulative Distribution Functions, 1975–92

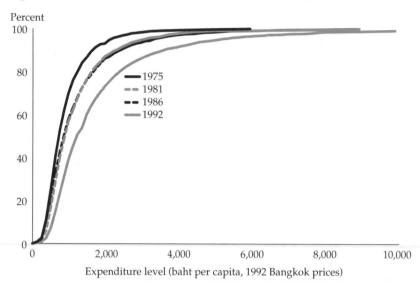

Expenditure level (baht per capita, 1992 Bangkok prices)

about rises in social welfare. If distribution function A lies nowhere above and somewhere below that of B, then A displays first-order dominance over B, and a theorem attributed to Saposnik (1981) establishes that any social welfare function that is individualistic and increasing in income will record an unambiguously higher level of social welfare in A than in B, regardless of its particular distributional judgments. Thailand's economic growth during 1975–92 was so rapid that it often succeeded in raising social welfare even by this demanding criterion, despite rising inequality (figures 4.6 and 4.7). The last year in the sample, 1992, displays first-order stochastic dominance over every previous year in the study. In addition, 1981 dominates 1975.

As the detail of the low-income range of the distribution functions in figure 4.7 shows, the picture with respect to 1986 is not so clear. The distribution functions for 1986 and 1975 cross just below the poverty line, while those for 1986 and 1981 cross well above it (not in the figure). This explains the lack of welfare dominance between those years. The increase in social welfare from the beginning to the end of the period is nevertheless remarkable. Incomes rose so much that, despite growing disparities, social welfare increased unambiguously between 1975 and 1992, as demonstrated by the significance of the first-order dominance results. These results, including the crossing between 1981 and 1986, are consistent with the evolution of poverty described in table 4.1.

Which economic mechanisms explain the sharp rise in Thai inequality between 1975 and 1992? We suggested earlier that at least two basic

Figure 4.7 Thailand: Cumulative Distribution Functions, Detail of Low-Income Range, 1975–92

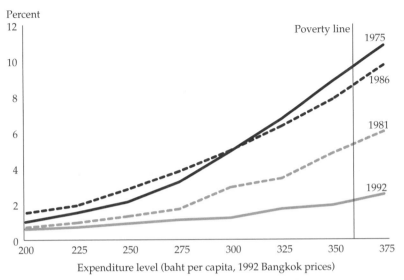

Expenditure level (baht per capita, 1992 Bangkok prices)

mechanisms seemed to be at work: growing spatial disparity in economic prosperity and increased dispersion in the returns accruing to different education levels and across different occupations or sectors of economic activity. The Thai case provides at least tentative backing for these hypotheses, particularly if we examine how household characteristics such as region of residence or education of the household head might explain inequality. The generalized entropy class of measures can be decomposed into two components: one that captures the inequality between the groups into which the population is partitioned and one that captures within-group inequality (appendix A). The share of total inequality accounted for by the between-group component (R_B) is often interpreted as the share of inequality explained by the particular attribute that defines the partition.

In the decomposition exercise that follows, we define our partitions according to the same characteristics used to construct the poverty profile: region, location of residence (urban or rural), socioeconomic class of the household, and characteristics of the household head (gender, age, and education). For the three measures $E(0)$, $E(1)$, and $E(2)$, table 4.4 shows the fraction of inequality that can be "explained" by the given characteristics or partitions in 1975 and 1992. While the results are suggestive, they should be interpreted with caution: no partition controls for any other attribute, and it is impossible to infer causality from these associations.

The explanatory power of each characteristic is smallest for the $E(2)$ measure, which is the most sensitive to higher incomes. Thus we focus our discussion on $E(0)$ and $E(1)$. The results in table 4.4 suggest that the gender and age of the household head explain little of the inequality in 1975, and this does not change much with time. The urban or rural location of residence explains 17–18 percent of the inequality in 1975, and the region of residence explains 14–15 percent. The explanatory power of both variables increases substantially over time: in 1992 the location of residence explains 28–29 percent of the inequality and the region of residence explains between 25–27 percent. In both cases this suggests that the spatial dimension of inequality is gaining importance in Thailand.

The education of the household head also explains 15–16 percent of the inequality in 1975, and the explanatory power of this variable doubles in 1992. A household's socioeconomic class has the most explanatory power. The portion of inequality explained by this factor is 25–27 percent in 1975, increasing to 35–39 percent in 1992. Once again, these increases suggest that there must be mechanisms at work affecting the pattern of returns to education and the sectoral structure of earnings in the Thai labor market. These transformations and any policy implications arising from them ought to be of considerable interest to those concerned with income distribution and welfare in Thailand. Finally, the explanatory power of all the characteristics combined is 58–59 percent in 1975, rising to 69 percent in 1992. This is quite a high overall share by international standards (see Cowell and Jenkins 1995; Ferreira and Litchfield 1997; and World Bank 1997d).

To summarize, the region and location of household residence, the socioeconomic (occupational) status of the household, and the education of the household head are important factors in the static decom-

Table 4.4 Thailand: Static Inequality Decomposition Results (R_B), 1975 and 1992

Variable	1975			1992		
	E(0)	E(1)	E(2)	E(0)	E(1)	E(2)
Region	0.153	0.135	0.070	0.265	0.254	0.155
Urban/rural	0.176	0.168	0.090	0.293	0.276	0.164
Socioeconomic class	0.271	0.248	0.138	0.390	0.348	0.206
Gender	0.004	0.003	0.002	0.006	0.005	0.003
Age	0.007	0.006	0.003	0.015	0.013	0.006
Education	0.149	0.160	0.106	0.307	0.328	0.235
All[a]	0.589	0.577	0.411	0.695	0.692	0.560

a. The partition by "all" attributes superimposes all previous partitions simultaneously. It is a gauge of joint explanatory power.
Source: Authors' calculations from Socioeconomic Survey data.

positions of inequality in 1975, and their explanatory power increases significantly by 1992. These results are consistent with increasing concentrations of poverty along the same lines.

While static decompositions are helpful in identifying some of the factors that explain inequality levels, they are less suited to understanding changes in inequality over time. To that end, we now turn to the results from a dynamic decomposition of E(0) proposed by Mookherjee and Shorrocks (1982). Appendix A discusses the decomposition in greater detail, and table 4.5 presents the results. The total change in the inequality measure E(0) can be decomposed into three distinct components. The first reflects changes in the composition (or population shares) of the different groups. The second component captures the influence of changes in the relative mean incomes of the groups. The third component is attributable to the impact of changes in inequality within the groups, and is often referred to as the pure inequality or unexplained effect. The greater is this residual term, the less important the attribute defining the partition is in explaining changes in inequality over time. In table 4.5 we present the results of the decompositions after dividing both sides by $\Delta E(0)$, so as to focus on proportional changes in inequality.

The results indicate that more than 40 percent of the change in E(0) can be accounted for by changes in mean income across regions. Changes in population share across regions do not help much in explaining increases in inequality. The picture is similar for decompositions by urban or rural location of residence. Changes in population share and relative income defined by age and sex of the household head did not contribute much to explaining the rise in inequality during 1975–92. In this respect, age and sex are clearly less important explanatory variables than regional or urban or rural location, education, or socioeconomic group.

Table 4.5 Thailand: Dynamic Inequality Decomposition Results (percent)

Variable	Population changes	Relative income	Residual
Region	3.17	42.23	55.76
Urban/rural	7.86	40.75	52.04
Socioeconomic class	16.93	47.59	33.49
Gender	0.60	0.79	98.63
Age	–0.92	2.65	98.47
Education	34.37	18.82	45.57

Note: The change in E(0) during 1975–92 was 0.133. The three effects may not add up to 100, because the formula is an approximation (see appendix A).
Source: Authors' calculations from Socioeconomic Survey data.

The dynamic decomposition by socioeconomic class shows that a little less than half of the total increase in inequality is a result of changes in relative mean incomes between the groups. The population effect accounts for another 17 percent of the total change. The effect of changes in population structure is most evident for the education of the household head, where it explains a third of the increase in inequality. This can be attributed mainly to a movement of individuals up the educational ladder, which has a positive net effect on inequality.

While much of the overall increase in inequality remains unexplained (see table 4.5, residual column), the dynamic decomposition does support earlier insights that spatial, educational, and occupational characteristics accounted for most of the change between 1975 and 1992. The decomposition tells us that, whereas regional, urban or rural, and sectoral factors act largely through growing disparities in relative mean incomes, education contributes to higher inequality both through a dispersion in means and through changes in the composition of the specific groups. Informative though this exercise may be, further research is clearly needed into the underlying causes of Thailand's increase in economic inequality.

5

Economic Policies, Poverty Reduction, and Equity

E ast Asia's economic policies have had a powerful influence on views about poverty reduction and equitable growth, since the region is a paragon of poverty reduction and has in the past been considered a paragon of equitable growth. Indeed, East Asia's success helped shape the perception, prevalent in the early 1990s, that parts of the developing world might not face an efficiency-equity tradeoff—that is, that a feasible set of policies was available that was good both for efficiency and rapid growth and for poverty reduction and equity. This chapter summarizes current thinking on policies to reduce poverty and then speculates on the implications of some of the new issues we have raised in this study.

Current Policy Paradigm

In assessing the effects of policies, it is useful to think of outcomes for both poverty and inequality in terms of the interaction between the capabilities of individuals and the opportunities they face (Sen 1985; World Bank 1990b). Poverty has fallen fastest when there has been rapid expansion both in the capabilities of the poor and in their opportunities. Similarly, changes in inequality reflect the interaction between changes in the distribution of capabilities and in the pattern of opportunities. Human capabilities are expanded largely through education and improved health; opportunities are expanded primarily when working individuals have access to land, capital, and new technologies to produce commodities that their societies or the world value. Transfers between individuals, or mediated by governments, also can affect poverty and inequality. While this may seem conceptually simple, the interactions among various economic policies and distributional outcomes in a general equilibrium framework are complex, and there is still much that we do not know about the effects specific policies have on poverty and inequality.

Growth and Poverty

The importance of economic growth for raising the incomes of the poor in East Asia cannot be overestimated. In general, since economic growth refers to rises in the mean of an income or expenditure distribution, and poverty reduction (as measured by the head-count) refers to a mass of that distribution moving above a certain threshold, poverty reduction should be determined by growth and changes in the dispersion of the distribution (inequality). This intuition has been formalized in a methodology developed by Datt and Ravallion (1992) that decomposes changes in poverty into two components: one for economic growth and one for distributional changes. The growth component measures the change in poverty by fixing the Lorenz curve at the reference date, allowing mean expenditure to grow, and computing the implied change in head-count. The redistribution component fixes mean expenditure at the reference date, allows the Lorenz curve to vary to reflect the actual change in inequality, and computes the resulting implied change in the head-count.[17] Denoting the poverty line by z, mean expenditure by μ, and the distribution of expenditures by Lorenz curve L, the poverty level at time t can be denoted as $P_t(z/\mu, L)$. Choosing the initial time period as the reference date, the change in poverty $P_T - P_0$ is decomposed as follows:

$$P_T - P_0 = P(z/\mu_T, L_0) - P(z/\mu_0, L_0) + P(z/\mu_0, L_T) - P(z/\mu_0, L_0) + \text{residual}$$
$$\text{(growth component)} \qquad \text{(redistribution component)}$$

The results of this decomposition for five countries in East Asia at different periods are presented in table 5.1. The growth component is not only always positive (as one would expect from the growth record), but also generally much larger than the redistribution component, which is more often negative than positive. Consequently, the growth component is often larger than the actual measured decline in the head-count index.

These results are consistent with the trend of increasing inequality described earlier, and with the fact that poverty continues to decline, despite this trend, because economic growth is sufficiently strong to outweigh the distributional effect. The exceptions to this picture are Malaysia (1973–89), the only country in our sample with a pronounced decline in inequality, Indonesia (1978–84), and the Philippines (1991–94). The most extreme case of a negative redistribution component was Thailand (1975–86), where the poverty-increasing effect of rising inequality overwhelmed positive growth and residual components, leading to an observed increased in poverty.[18] In general, however,

Table 5.1 Decomposition of Poverty Reduction into Growth and Redistribution Components

Economy	Period	Decline in head-count index (percentage points)	Growth component	Redistribution component	Residual
Malaysia	1973–89	19.1	16.4	3.9	−1.2
Thailand	1975–86	−1.9	6.1	−11.0	3.0
	1986–92	10.0	10.0	−1.5	1.5
Indonesia	1970–78	3.8	7.6	−2.7	−1.1
	1978–84	26.7	18.5	3.4	4.8
	1984–95	23.6	22.4	−3.1	4.3
China (rural)	1985–90	−2.1	2.4	−4.1	−0.4
	1990–93	2.2	5.9	−3.3	−0.4
Philippines	1985–88	5.0	5.2	−0.3	0.1
	1988–91	−1.2	2.9	−4.1	0.0
	1991–94	1.7	0.8	1.0	−0.1

Note: Declines are presented as positive entries; negative numbers indicate contributions to increasing poverty.
Source: Authors' calculations.

growth was sufficiently buoyant to more than compensate for greater dispersion and keep poverty reduction on track.[19]

Thus it is clear that the policies that helped East Asia achieve its remarkable sustained growth also deserve much of the credit for reducing poverty. Though prosperity may not have been growing at the same rate for everyone, it has been growing enough to lift many people out of extreme poverty.

The importance of economic growth for poverty reduction raises two policy-relevant questions: What factors explain East Asia's stellar overall growth performance? And what dimensions of policy influenced interactions between growth, inequality, and poverty?

Determinants of East Asian Growth

There has recently been a heated debate on whether East Asian growth was "miraculous." That terminology is probably unhelpful. But the region's growth has been unprecedented: no other large group of economies has sustained similar growth rates for three decades (somewhat less for China; significantly less for Indochina). The debate has revolved around whether growth can be explained purely in terms of traditional sources (human and physical capital accumulation) or whether increases in total factor productivity also played a role (Krugman 1994; Young 1994). The evidence favors the following explanation: East Asian savings and investment rates are exceptionally high by international standards. By and large, investment has been put to good use: any rise in capital-output ratios has been a consequence of a natural process of capital deepening. Both technological change and product upgrading have taken place throughout economies and in all sectors: agriculture, manufacturing, and services (Sarel forthcoming). China, emerging from its legacy of central planning, appears to have enjoyed unusually high productivity growth that contributed to its overall performance both within sectors and for the whole economy (Kraay 1996).

However, the real question is how East Asian economies got on and continued along the virtuous path of high savings and investment and rapid growth.[20] The answers appear to include a combination of external conditions and policy and institutional factors (ADB 1997). Two external conditions are worth emphasizing. The first is favorable geographic location: not just proximity to major coastal trading routes but also (especially for latecomers) being located in a growing, integrating, and constantly restructuring region. A second exogenous condition is the initial level of income. Other things being equal, low incomes relative to other economies, or "relative backwardness," is associated with faster growth, as followers catch up with leaders.[21] All East Asian economies started out relatively poor, and some still are. For most of the world other things have not been equal, and divergence, not convergence, has been the rule, hampering efforts to reduce poverty. East Asia managed to get other things better than equal, and this is where inherited and current policies matter. Poverty reduction and economic growth depend on policies that promote good education and health services; prudent macroeconomic management, based on sensible fiscal policies; international engagement through trade, investment, and acquisition of foreign ideas and technology; and effective institutions, including well-organized bureaucracies, well-functioning financial systems, and productive relationships between the public and private sectors (World Bank 1993a; Campos and Root 1996; Aoki and others 1996).

Policies That Influence the Distributional Pattern of Growth

The more relevant questions for this study concern how policies influence the pattern of growth in a way that involves the poor or contributes to equitable growth. It is useful to summarize thinking in terms of capabilities, opportunities, and transfers, but more important are the interactions among these factors—especially between rising capabilities and expanding opportunities (Birdsall and Sabot 1993).

Capabilities and human resource development. The aspect of East Asian policy that most contributed to equitable growth in capabilities was government financing and provisioning of basic social services. The story is particularly clear for education, where all East Asian societies made expansion of first primary and then secondary education a priority. Government provisioning partially solved credit constraints, particularly those faced by poor people in financing the education of their children. Significant contributions were also made by households, since the opportunity cost of schooling—as opposed to working—is often larger than the pecuniary cost. Across the region the demand for schooling was reflected in a rapid rise in enrollments once schools and teachers were made available. Financing was strongly biased toward lower levels of schooling. In the Republic of Korea, for example, government finance accounts for almost 100 percent of the direct costs of primary schooling, plummeting to less than 50 percent for tertiary education. Starting in the 1970s Indonesia used oil rents to fund a nationwide school-building campaign, resulting in a massive expansion in primary schooling, but much secondary and tertiary education and technical training remains privately financed (World Bank 1997c and forthcoming). Studies of expenditure incidence confirm that primary schooling had relatively equitable incidence in the 1980s (more equitable than income), and secondary and tertiary spending is relatively inequitable (van de Walle and Nead 1995).

Why does education matter for poverty and inequality? While the answer may seem obvious, there are in fact a number of influences. Most of the poor are rural dwellers that depend on agriculture. Direct effects of education on agricultural productivity are significant though not large—working, for example, by increasing the propensity to adopt new technologies. Probably of greater quantitative importance are the effects on participation in nonagricultural work: education encourages movement into better nonfarm rural work and migration to towns for industrial and service employment. A general finding from high- and middle-income countries was that expanding the relative supply of education tends to reduce earnings inequality. Consider Korea, where the large expansion in relatively educated workers was the most important source of a substantial compression in earnings differentials among workers between 1970 and 1990 (Kim and Topel 1995). Educational expansion was much more equal in Korea than in Brazil, which helps explain Brazil's greater earnings inequality (Park, Ross, and Sabot 1996).

Education also has significant indirect effects. For example, educated mothers are more likely than uneducated ones to ensure that their children receive an education and live healthily (World Bank 1993a; Birdsall and Sabot 1993). And as we have seen, households with higher incomes are more likely to send their children to school.

The health situation is more complex. Policy usually focuses on health services, though these form only part of the equation influencing health outcomes, with education and income of at least equal importance. In most East Asian societies a significant amount of spending on health services—sometimes more than half—is private and not public, reflecting a substantial private demand for such services and limited public coverage. Nevertheless, some core interventions to improve health outcomes, especially those that tackle infectious diseases, including through improved water and sanitation, have a strong rationale for public intervention, and are particularly beneficial to the poor. Incidence analysis further indicates that the most basic health services, often through rural health centers that provide preventive and curative care, tend to be much more equally distributed than incomes or higher levels of services.

Finally, education, health, and incomes all appear to bring second-round gains for poverty, and in some conditions inequality, by contributing to demographic transition. Despite the dearth of quantitative work in this area, at least two channels of influence are evident. First, a sharp reduction in the dependency ratio for the school-age population greatly reduces the public and private spending required to sustain a steady rise in educational attainment. For example, Korea has vastly increased its education spending per pupil, both from public and private sources, with a small and roughly constant share of spending as a share of GDP (most African countries spend much less per pupil but much more as a share of GDP). Second, a reduction in the size of new cohorts of workers helps tighten labor markets, which has sustained wage increases and tended to favor unskilled (and relatively poorer) workers, at least during some phases of economic development.

Patterns of expanding opportunities. In general, rising capabilities due to better health and educational outcomes improve welfare directly (Drèze and Sen 1989). But they can also translate into higher incomes, provided there is a context of rising economic opportunities. In East Asia poverty-reducing growth was promoted by policy choices and institutional structures that favored shared rural growth and expanded industrial and service employment. Transfers, mostly private, also have played a role.

As noted, poverty in East Asia is still predominantly a rural phenomenon. Almost all East Asian societies are a long way from the transition most of Latin America experienced in the 1980s, when the poor became concentrated in urban areas. A rise in agricultural productivity was the most important factor behind poverty reduction in East Asia, especially for low-income economies. The rise was driven by three factors: land management structures, technology, and public policy (Binswanger, Deininger, and Feder 1993; Teranishi 1996).

- *Relatively equal land distribution.* Whether because of significant land reforms (China, Japan, Korea, Taiwan (China), and Vietnam) or the historic absence of concentrated farming (Indonesia, Malaysia, and Thailand), land is reasonably equally distributed in East Asia; much more so than in Latin America. Also important is the predominance of family farming as an organizational form, by far the most efficient means of organizing labor in most categories of farming. These two phenomena created the political and technical conditions for efficient and (relatively) equitable agricultural growth.

- *Technological change.* Rural development in the past few decades has been powerfully influenced by the green revolution, which created the technological preconditions for sustained productivity increases in agriculture. Thus East Asia's most labor-intensive sector has been a source of growth in internal productivity. This is in sharp contrast to the situation in England and the United States during their early industrialization. In both countries relatively stagnant technological change in agriculture—in contrast to the dynamism of industry—slowed poverty reduction and fueled rises in inequality (Williamson and Polak 1990).

- *Support for farming through pricing policy and provision of rural public goods.* Avoiding overprotection for industry and overvaluation of exchange rates was important to maintaining reasonable incentives for agricultural production. By one analysis, Malaysia's direct and indirect taxation of agriculture amounted to less than 20 percent, and Thailand's to 40 percent, compared with more than 50 percent for Côte d'Ivoire and Ghana. Perhaps of greater importance than pricing effects was governments' direct action to provide the roads, research, and extension services needed to raise agricultural productivity and provide access to markets (Teranishi 1996).

China illustrates the interaction among these factors. In the 1950s land reform led to a major equalization of landholdings, followed by collectivization, which resulted in low agricultural productivity. Between 1979 and 1984 a combination of the shift to family farming, improved incentives through pricing policy, and continued support in terms of roads and agricultural services led to extraordinary growth in agricultural productivity. Village land allocation mechanisms distributed land on the basis of household labor availability, with strong equity consequences. However, there is some evidence of negative efficiency effects from tenurial insecurity (see box 2.2). Once the one-time gains in productivity were achieved and the terms of trade shifted against agriculture as a result of government pricing policy, agricultural growth slowed, linked increasingly to shifts in product mix, growth in nonfarm markets, and technological upgrading.

The second development central to reducing poverty in East Asia was rapid employment growth in the rural nonfarm sector and in urban areas. These employment transformations were immense. In the late 1950s less than 30 percent of Malaysia's workforce was in wage-paying industrial and service jobs; by the late 1980s this share had risen to 60 percent. In Korea agricultural employment fell from 50 percent of the workforce in 1970 to 20 percent in the late 1980s. Aggregate economic growth was a powerful force behind these developments, but four other factors contributed to the strong positive interactions: agricultural growth itself, opening up to international markets, avoidance of dualism in factor markets, and interaction between education and modern employment.

- *Agriculture and rural nonfarm employment.* Growth in rural nonfarm employment opportunities has been a major feature of rural income growth, helping to absorb workers from lower-productivity farming. This growth has been driven by a robust agriculture and improved rural economic infrastructure. Higher agricultural incomes have increased the demand for goods and services and helped finance off-farm investments (with input supplies playing a secondary role). Rural infrastructure both provides employment in the construction phase and reduces the costs of rural commerce. Rural Java (Indonesia) experienced a transport revolution and a burst of rural nonfarm and peripheral urban employment in the late 1970s and early 1980s. This was the result of steady growth in rice incomes and direct and indirect government spending on schools, roads, and other rural infrastructure. Rural nonfarm employment in China grew by 130 million jobs between 1980 and 1995, when total agricultural employment showed no growth, and total urban employment rose by 70 million jobs. Township and village enterprises were a major part of this expansion, driven initially by the sharp growth in agricultural incomes and later by national and international linkages.
- *Openness and employment.* Openness to international exchange and technology has many beneficial effects, notably on employment. The opening of industry to a virtually unlimited international market

releases the domestic employment market from an exclusive dependence on growth in domestic demand in a relatively closed economy, and provides a market base for urban-based growth in services.

- *Avoidance of dualism.* All societies have marked differences between earnings in different activities that are only partly linked to the (apparent) differences in the capabilities of individuals. Other things being equal, earnings are generally higher in urban jobs in large firms, for example. East Asia is no exception to this rule, but the extent of such apparent dualism is relatively modest in most economies. Highly paid protected jobs were avoided as a result of relatively open product markets, avoidance of severe distortions in allocating financial resources, and at least de facto absence of extreme protection or large wage differentials for favored groups of workers. China is the most important exception, with relatively large urban-rural differentials, a rather weakly integrated national labor market, and some 100 million state enterprise workers who receive substantial social security and other benefits. There, employment growth in "modern" enterprises has been slow relative to capital expansion.

- *Education and "modern" employment.* The equalizing effects of educational expansion can be partly explained by the interaction between shifting patterns of demand and supply of labor. In East Asia rising educational attainment effectively anticipated demands coming from the modern sector. As industry has upgraded from labor-intensive toys and garments, through semiskilled electronics assembly, to highly skilled engineering, electronics, and heavy industry, demand has shifted from primary to secondary and college educated workers. A parallel rise in educational demand has occurred in the service sectors. In most East Asian economies educational expansion took place ahead of demand, delivering new cohorts of appropriately skilled workers for each phase of industrialization. This allowed rising average wages to be underwritten by growing productivity, and moderate or declining wage differentials. As noted above, this trend may now be shifting, especially in the region's middle- and upper-income economies.

Transfers were a third tool used to reduce poverty and inequality in East Asia. Private income transfers, especially within families, are the most common way in which East Asians deal with financial insecurity arising from ill health, disablement, unemployment, or old age. In particular, private transfers have enabled the elderly to share in overall income increases. Apart from in-kind provision of social and economic services, public transfers have been unimportant. There are a few exceptions: China's state enterprise sector; the publicly managed, though individually funded, provident funds of Malaysia and Singapore; and selected transfers to reduce the effects of recession (for example, local public works in Korea in 1979–81; see Drèze and Sen 1989, and management of rice prices to reduce consumption declines in Malaysia in 1984–87). As we argue below, this modest role for monetary public transfers may well be about to change.

Policy and the New Issues in Poverty and Inequality

For many of the poor in East Asia today, continued development through broadly based growth and expansion in basic services will be the most effective way of improving incomes and living standards. However, the trend toward poverty concentration and the signs in some economies of rising inequality should be cause for vigilance among policymakers. What do these new developments imply for policy?

Economies in Transition from Central Planning

In the former Soviet Union and Eastern Europe issues of poverty and inequality are driven by the demise of old transfer and employment systems and the collapse in production and incomes that most economies passed through. East Asia's transition economies are mostly different. Poverty is mainly rural, there has been no transitional collapse (outside Mongolia), economies were not overindustrialized, and the relative decline in state employment is being rapidly mopped up by nonstate employment. Pursuit of strategies pioneered by early East Asian successes is a good bet for poverty reduction and equity. For example, if Vietnam could follow a path similar to that of Indonesia (Java in particular) in the 1970s and 1980s, the welfare of the poor would improve substantially.

There are four exceptions, and they raise four questions:

- *Mongolia was an inefficient, overindustrialized, Soviet-style welfare state.* It is going through a severe transitional decline in output owing to loss of markets and subsidies and reduced income transfers. Mongolia's only hope is a growth recovery. Meanwhile, can special attention be given to equity, perhaps involving transitional transfers to households facing losses?
- *Health care provision.* In China and Vietnam in particular, there has been a significant reduction in village- and commune-based mechanisms of health provisioning and insurance, with partial replacement by private means. Some of this makes sense, but is additional public action needed to tackle the market failures in health care provision?

- *China's social security provisions.* China's state enterprise workers have extensive social security, financed on a pay-as-you-go basis, at the enterprise or city level. Social security has to be rolled back to support enterprise restructuring. What alternative mechanisms can be introduced to meet the implicit past contract with workers and to design efficient means of providing for old age, ill health, disability, and unemployment?
- *China's wage and employment structures.* China's labor market historically has had highly compressed differentials across skills and between genders. Today some decompression with respect to skills is taking place—a desirable development, except for risks of a rising gender gap driven by cultural biases favoring men. China also has a highly segmented labor market. Will internal equity and labor market stability be best served by encouraging or controlling migration?

Inequality

Many East Asian societies are voicing concern about high or rising inequality. From a policy perspective it might be useful, if somewhat artificial, to divide the issues between those at the bottom, in the middle, and at the top of the income distribution.

At the bottom the primary concern is with individuals or groups that may be left out of the development process or reap little benefit from national gains. The three main groups appear to be:
- Those in poor areas: is there scope for more spatially based targeting of programs to address the concentration of poverty in certain areas, along the lines of the INPRES Desa Tertinggal targeted assistance program in Indonesia?
- Ethnic groups: is there a case for additional subsidies or special kinds of social action to strengthen the capabilities of disadvantaged ethnic groups and increase their participation in national growth?
- The economically inactive: will the disabled, sick, and elderly (not least the future old in one-child China) fall through the net of informal and formal transfer mechanisms?

In the middle of the income distribution, some economies are showing signs of a shift in the old dynamic equilibrium, in which the expanding supply of skills matched growing demand. Should the balance of education spending change in response to the increasing wage differentials at higher skill levels? Should special action be taken to deal with mid-career workers whose skills become obsolete? Should international migration be managed to protect the wages of unskilled workers in receiving countries?

At the top of the distribution there are increasingly visible cases of large-scale wealth, as illustrated by the rising number of East Asian multimillionaires. Here the concern appears to be with unfair wealth acquisition linked to state–private family elite relations, lack of transparency, corruption, and rents. Large-scale privatization and private involvement in infrastructure investment may provide fertile ground for unfair wealth acquisition and rent-seeking behavior in the future. Would a strategy favoring competition and transparency effectively tackle these concerns?

Household Insecurity

East Asia is on the cusp of a massive transition to urbanized, aging societies, a transition likely to proceed at a pace without historical precedent. Should governments abandon their resolve to preserve family-based social support systems and provide more generous safety nets of their own? How can social insurance mechanisms reduce household risks without contributing to Latin American–style crises in social security funding or European-style labor market rigidities? Where in the continuum from universal entitlements to highly targeted interventions should they locate?

6
Conclusions

In revisiting the evolution of poverty and inequality in East Asia over the past two decades, this study has come up with four main findings.

First, the remarkable and sustained rates of economic growth throughout most of the region have generated considerable benefits for the poor. Focusing on absolute poverty, defined at a $1 a day poverty line, we found substantial reductions in both the incidence and depth of poverty almost everywhere. The Philippines reduced poverty at a much slower rate than other economies, as it also had a slower growth rate in per capita GDP. In Lao PDR, Mongolia, and Vietnam poverty was much more widespread than in the rest of our sample, but indirect evidence suggests that poverty reduction rates, particularly in Vietnam, became promising in the late 1980s. China, Indonesia, Malaysia, and Thailand have experienced absolute reductions in poverty over the past twenty years that are exceptional by any international or historical standard. As a result East Asia's share in the pool of the world's poorest people continues to shrink. While the 350 million East Asians who fall below the $1 a day poverty line still account for about a third of the world's poor, this share has been declining steadily.

Our second finding stems from the different experiences of East Asian economies and relates to a change in the map of poverty within the region. As a result of rapid, sustained growth and poverty reduction, richer countries such as Malaysia, Thailand, and presumably Korea have relatively few people left who subsist on less than $1 a day. This is not to say that poverty has been eliminated in these countries, and indeed they generally have adopted higher standards for themselves, raising the income level deemed to be an appropriate poverty threshold. As our case study of Thailand demonstrates, while poverty is negligible at the $1 a day line, the 1992 head-count for the $2 a day line was 16 percent. Nevertheless, since there are still some 350 million people in the region below the more stringent $1 a day line, we restricted our international comparisons to this case and found a reduction in the share of regional poverty not only for Malaysia and Thailand but also for Indonesia (from 10 percent in 1985 to 6 percent in 1995). Lao PDR, Mongolia, Papua New Guinea, and the Philippines saw increases in their shares of the region's poor. China's share edged up to just over three-quarters of the number of poor people in the region. While the changing poverty map is a natural consequence of different rates of growth and poverty reduction, it does signal the need to focus attention on the specific needs of lagging economies, many of which are in transition.

Our third finding is that poverty remains unevenly distributed within most East Asian economies. In Thailand, where we were able to investigate changes over time, the evidence suggests a tendency toward greater concentration of poverty among groups traditionally most vulnerable to it. East Asian poverty remains principally a rural phenomenon, and it continues to affect farmers and the uneducated disproportionately. In some countries, such as Vietnam, poverty also varies considerably among ethnic groups. In Thailand poverty head-counts have generally fallen for all groups, but proportionally less for those with higher initial values. As a result the poor have become more concentrated in rural areas, especially among agriculturists; in areas with much higher poverty head-counts, such as Thailand's northeast; and among people with little or no education.

Our fourth finding casts some doubt on the perception of East Asia as an atypically egalitarian region. According to the best data sets, East Asia is indeed more equal than Latin America or Sub-Saharan Africa, and on par with the average for the Middle East and North Africa. But it is less equal than the average for industrial countries, Eastern Europe, or South Asia. Moreover, it appears that after a period of stability or decline, inequality appears to be on the rise in some economies. This trend is most notable in China, Hong Kong (China), and Thailand, but there is anecdotal evidence that it may be more general. While an empirical analysis of its causes lies outside the scope of this study, two likely hypotheses are suggested: one, that the rate of increase in the demand for more skilled workers outstripped the rate of increase in their supply, raising earnings differentials across some education levels and occupations; and two, that disparity in the spatial distribution of economic prosperity, which can be measured across regions or between urban and rural areas in many economies, is rising. Static and dynamic decompositions of inequality across population groups in Thailand offer tentative support for both hypotheses.

While it would be inappropriate to consider specific country policy issues in a regional study such as this one, the general implications of these broad findings were briefly discussed. The evidence is strong enough that it warrants reiterating the obvious: there is no doubt that maintaining an environment conducive to economic growth is beneficial to the poor. For all but one of the economies for which we have data, a decomposition between an effect due to growth and one due to redistribution found not only that growth was most important to poverty reduction, but also that redistribution components alone generally counteracted it. The growth component exceeded the net effect in many cases. Macroeconomic stability, investment in human and physical capital, limits on microeconomic distortions, and openness to trade, capital flows, and ideas are all tested ingredients in the East Asian growth recipe. They should not be tinkered with where they are well established, and they should be introduced where they are not.

More specifically, some policies are particularly effective in improving the living standards of the poor because they either augment their capabilities or expand their opportunities. Policies that build up the human capital of the poor, such as public investment in primary and secondary education, basic health care, and water and sanitation, are examples of the first. Policies leading to more equal land distribution and public provision of rural infrastructure enlarge their opportunities. So do policies that encourage the growth of employment in services and manufacturing.

Moving beyond proven policy implications, some of our findings raised new questions for governments and donors alike. We have not attempted to answer these here, but they would be interesting foci for future research. Three broad areas merit exploration. The first concerns the problems of economic transition from a centrally planned to a market system. The problems are clearly different in Mongolia, which is experiencing a decline in output similar to that in the former Soviet Union, than in Cambodia, Lao PDR, and Vietnam. China, on the other hand, must address issues related to the management of health and social security and to state enterprise employment.

The second area to explore is rising inequality and its implications. Is this an issue that governments should address at all? If so, how can it be tackled with the least efficiency cost? Should existing policies toward migration, internal or external, be revisited? We suggest a renewed policy focus on poor areas, since our findings indicate greater spatial concentration of poverty as well as greater regional inequality. In addition, the skill composition of the labor force calls for attention from education and employment specialists.

The third area to explore is household insecurity. Are households in fact more vulnerable than in the past? If so, is it feasible to consider public action to complement private and family-based support networks? Do demographic trends and rising urbanization add weight to arguments for greater public transfers or for formal systems of social insurance?

The answers to any of these questions require much deeper analysis than is possible in a comparative survey such as this. There is considerable scope for conceptual and empirical research, some of which is already under way. In any event, the evidence suggests that these are the right questions to ask if East Asia is to continue its remarkable progress in reducing poverty and improving living conditions for its people.

Appendix A
Data and Methodology

A ll the poverty measures reported in table 2.1 originate from house-hold survey data. The information was generally made available to us in grouped form: for example, cumulative proportions of income or expenditure accruing to various percentiles of the distribution, income ranges with associated densities, and so on. Incomes and expenditure values, measured in local currency, were deflated to 1985 prices using the best available consumer price index. For China separate rural and urban consumer price indexes were obtained from the *China Statistical Yearbook* and applied separately to deflate rural and urban expenditures. For other economies we lacked data on rural and urban indexes and therefore used the World Bank national consumer price index as the deflator.

Figures were then converted into dollars using 1985 purchasing power parity exchange rates from Summers and Heston (1991). The grouped data were used to generate parametric estimates of Lorenz curves using POVCAL, a software program developed by Martin Ravallion, Shaohua Chen, and Gaurav Datt at the World Bank. A Lorenz curve plots the cumulative share of income or expenditure for a distribution against the cumulative population share. Two parametric specifications for the Lorenz curve that have good empirical approximation records are the Beta, proposed by Kakwani (1980), and the General Quadratic, proposed by Villaseñor and Arnold (1989). From the grouped data POVCAL estimates the appropriate parameters for both specifications and indicates which one best fits the data. The program, designed to produce poverty and inequality estimates, was ideal for our needs.[22] The method is obviously less accurate than using household-level unit-record data, but given the limited access to that data, POVCAL has proved a useful tool for poverty monitoring in many instances.

Our specific data sources and some methodological exceptions are noted below:

- For Indonesia data on expenditure distributions for 1975–84 is obtained from the *Statistical Yearbook of Indonesia* for various years. *The Statistical Yearbook* publishes population data grouped by expenditure decile (POVCAL type 2) along with mean expenditure. For

1987, 1993, and 1995 data are derived directly from unit-record data from the National Household Survey of Indonesia, popularly known as SUSENAS. For these years data are in POVCAL type 5 form.

- Data for Lao PDR, Mongolia, Papua New Guinea, the Philippines, and Thailand are in POVCAL type 5 form and are derived from national consumption surveys (Lao PDR Expenditure and Consumption Survey for Lao PDR, Living Standards Measurement Survey for Mongolia, 1996 Household Survey of Papua New Guinea for Papua New Guinea, Family Income and Expenditure Survey for the Philippines, and Thailand Socioeconomic Survey for Thailand).

- We did not have data on expenditure distributions at the national level for China or Malaysia. Lorenz curves for these countries were obtained using income distribution, but for China the mean of the distribution was set equal to the mean consumption to estimate consumption poverty. Since we had no information on the savings patterns of the poor in Malaysia, we made the conservative assumption of no savings or dissavings below the poverty line for that country. The estimates for Malaysia, therefore, are a measure of income poverty. (These methodological choices are further justified in the next subsection.)

- Vietnam's expenditure distribution is derived from the 1993 Living Standards Measurement Survey. However, neither purchasing power parity exchange rates nor a consumer price index are available for Vietnam from standard sources. We estimated the purchasing power parity exchange rate for 1993 by regressing the differences between nominal U.S. dollar exchange rates and purchasing power parity exchange rates on per capita income (expressed in U.S. dollars) and secondary school enrollment rates for a cross-section of low-income countries and applying the coefficients to Vietnam. According to our estimate the 1993 U.S. dollar exchange rate for Vietnam was about 4.5 times the purchasing power parity exchange rate. Using this conversion coefficient, local currency expenditures were converted to purchasing power parity dollar expenditures and then deflated to 1985 price levels using the U.S. consumer price index.

Once the estimated Lorenz curve has been chosen, along with an estimate of mean household consumption expenditure per capita for each distribution, poverty can be estimated as follows. Because its first derivative at percentile p is the ratio of income accruing to that percentile to overall mean income, $L'(p) = y/\mu(y)$, the Lorenz curve can be used to obtain the estimate of the head-count: $L'(H) = z/\mu(y)$, once the poverty line and the mean of the distribution are known. The head-count estimates in table 2.1 are derived in this way. The estimated absolute number of poor people in each economy is simply the product of the head-count and the population at the relevant time. The poverty gap is the product of the head-count and the average distance between the incomes of the poor and the poverty line, estimated from grouped data.

Furthermore, in the Philippines in 1975 and in Lao PDR, Malaysia, Mongolia, and Papua New Guinea in 1985 no distributional data were available for any year sufficiently close to the comparison date. The values entered (in italics) for these cases were obtained by scaling down the distribution mean analyzed for an economy for a later year by a factor equal to the compounded growth rate in the interval between the two dates. The growth rate used was for consumption from the two closest household surveys. For economies for which only one household survey was available, we used the average annual growth rate of private consumption from the economy's national accounts. The Lorenz curve was assumed unchanged, which implies perfectly distribution-neutral growth. While these numbers are less reliable than the other entries, this assumption is partially validated by the fact that distributional changes over time are often quite small relative to differences across countries (Deininger and Squire 1996). As a result the redistribution components of changes in poverty for the economies in our sample were generally small relative to the growth components (see table 5.1). The alternative would have been simply to avoid any intertemporal comparison for these countries. For Vietnam, however, the head-count and the poverty gap index for 1985, obtained from Dollar and Litvack (forthcoming), are based on the assumption that the distribution may have worsened during the past decade. The head-count in 1985 is based on a Gini index of 0.30, in 1993 on a Gini index of 0.34.

Finally, the regional totals presented in the first row of table 2.1 were derived as follows: The row for East Asia gives the total number of poor people for economies *in the table*. The 1975 entries for Lao PDR, Mongolia, Papua New Guinea, and Vietnam were estimated by further extrapolating the mean from subsequent growth rates, as described above. Since the estimates become increasingly suspect as they stray from the original distribution, they are not reported for the economies themselves but rather are added to the regional total to allow for a general idea of the trend over time. Head-counts and poverty gaps are weighted averages, with weights equal to an economy's population as a share of the total regional population.

Estimating the Head-count Index
Without the Expenditure Distribution

As described above, because unit-record data are not available, the head-count indexes in this study are derived from estimated Lorenz curves, given the fact that $L'(H) = z/\mu$. In general, the ideal head-count is the expenditure head-count, derived from the Lorenz curve associated with the distribution of consumption expenditures (and from mean expenditure). However, in some cases—such as China and Malaysia in our sample—rather than expenditure distributions, income distributions (and mean income) are available, along with a value for mean consumption expenditure, usually from national accounts data.

In those cases, two alternative approaches exist for estimating the ideal expenditure head-count. The first is to compute an income head-count from mean income and the Lorenz curve associated with the income distribution; the second is to compute an adjusted head-count by relying on the income Lorenz curve but using the mean consumption expenditure. Which of these two approaches yields a better estimate for the expenditure head-count?

It depends on two factors: the relationship between mean income and expenditure; and the relative slopes of the two Lorenz curves in the vicinity of the expenditure head-count. That is, it depends on the relationship between savings at the poverty line and average savings in the economy. If there is reason to believe that the savings rate at the poverty line is greater than the average savings rate, then the adjusted head-count will provide a better estimator. The alternative case, when savings at the poverty line are lower than average savings, is much more likely to be observed in practice. If it occurs, then the income head-count is likely (though not certain) to provide a better estimate. As the examples of China and Thailand demonstrate empirically, both sub-cases of the latter case can occur in practice.

Definitions

Let x_i denote the consumption expenditure and y_i the income of individual i. Let z be the poverty line, and bold type denote the population vectors. Let L_E denote the Lorenz curves associated with the expenditure distribution $F(x)$ and L_Y the Lorenz curves associated with the income distribution $G(y)$. Analogously, let expenditure mean $\mu(x):= \mu_E$ and income mean $\mu(y) := \mu_Y$.

Given these functions and parameters, note that

- The expenditure head-count H_E is given implicitly by $L_E'(H_E) = z/\mu_E$.
- The income head-count H_Y is given implicitly by $L_Y'(H_Y) = z/\mu_Y$.
- The adjusted head-count H_A is given implicitly by $L_Y'(H_A) = z/\mu_E$.

The question then is whether H_A or H_Y is a better estimator for H_E. Clearly, it follows from the second and third statements above that the two will be identical when $\mu_Y = \mu_E$. The general case, however, is that

$\mu_Y > \mu_E$. (We do not consider the case when $\mu_Y < \mu_E$ because of empirical irrelevance.)

Proposition

When $\mu_Y > \mu_E$, two cases may arise:
(i) If $L_E'(H_E) < L_Y'(H_E)$, then $H_E > H_A > H_Y$.
(ii) If, on the other hand, $L_E'(H_E) > L_Y'(H_E)$, then $H_E < H_A$ and $H_Y < H_A$.

PROOF.   (i) $L_E'(H_E) < L_Y'(H_E)$ and
$L_Y'(H_A) = L_E'(H_E)$ from the first and third statements above.
So $L_Y'(H_A) < L_Y'(H_E)$.
Since $L_Y'' > 0$ over the domain [0,1], it follows that $H_A < H_E$.
Since $\mu_Y > \mu_E$, $L_Y'(H_Y) = z/\mu_Y < z/\mu_E = L_Y'(H_A)$.
Since $L_Y'' > 0$ over the domain [0,1], it follows that $H_Y < H_A$.
Hence $H_Y < H_A < H_E$, as we set out to prove.

(ii) $L_E'(H_E) > L_Y'(H_E)$ and
$L_Y'(H_A) = L_E'(H_E)$ from the first and third statements above.
So $L_Y'(H_A) > L_Y'(H_E)$.
Since $L_Y'' > 0$ over the domain [0,1], it follows that $H_A > H_E$.
Since $\mu_Y > \mu_E$, $L_Y'(H_Y) = z/\mu_Y < z/\mu_E = L_Y'(H_A)$.
Since $L_Y'' > 0$ over the domain [0,1], it follows that $H_Y < H_A$.
Hence $H_E < H_A$ and $H_Y < H_A$, as we set out to prove.

To interpret these findings, note that the key condition on the slope of the income and expenditure Lorenz curves can be rewritten as follows. The condition for case (i), $L_E'(H_E) < L_Y'(H_E)$, can be rewritten as $z/\mu_E < y(z)/\mu_Y$, where $y(z)$ is the income accruing to the person on percentile H_E, that is, the income accruing to someone whose consumption expenditure is equal to the poverty line z. This can be rewritten as $\mu_Y/\mu_E < y(z)/z$, or $s_p > s$, where s is the average savings rate and s_p is the savings rate at the income level that generates consumption expenditure z. Conversely, case (ii) occurs when $s_p < s$. In case (i) it is clear that both income and adjusted head-counts will underestimate the true expenditure head-count, and that the adjusted head-count will always have a smaller bias and thus be the better estimator.

In case (ii) it is impossible to be categorical. The adjusted head-count will always overestimate the true expenditure head-count, but the income head-count may overestimate it, underestimate it, or be equal to it. What we do know is that if the income head-count also overestimates it, like the adjusted head-count it will do so by less, and thus be a better estimator.

As we have seen, the condition for case (i)—a higher than average savings rate at the poverty line—seems unlikely to hold empirically. Indeed, case (ii), which holds whenever mean income exceeds mean expenditure and the average savings rate of the economy exceeds the savings rate at the poverty line, can reasonably be held ex ante to be the most likely. Furthermore, the probability that the absolute value of the difference between the income head-count and the true expenditure head-count exceeds the difference between the adjusted head-count and expenditure head-count can reasonably be expected to be low, since that can only happen if H_Y is below H_E by an amount greater than $(H_A - H_E)$. It might therefore be argued that, in the absence of any information on the expenditure distribution other than its mean, the income head-count H_Y should be used rather than the adjusted head-count H_A to estimate H_E.

Nevertheless, the reverse can hold in practice. We found this by examining per capita income and per capita expenditure distributions in Thailand for 1988 and in rural China for 1992, producing three estimates: the expenditure head-count (H_E) using the per capita expenditure distribution and its mean; the income head-count (H_Y), using the income distribution and its mean; and the adjusted head-count (H_A), using the income distribution and the expenditure mean. The simulation results are quite revealing (table A.1).

These results provide interesting empirical illustrations of the two possibilities for case ii. Both Thailand and rural China are clearly examples of case (ii): $H_E < H_A$ and $H_Y < H_A$. But because $H_E < H_Y$ in Thailand, the income head-count is a better estimator of the expenditure head-count than is the adjusted value. In rural China H_Y was so far below H_A that its downward bias with respect to H_E exceeded the upward bias of H_A. In this case the adjusted head-count is a better estimator.

Table A.1 China and Thailand: Alternative Methods of Estimating Poverty Measures

Method	Estimated head-count index	
	Rural China, 1992	Thailand, 1988
Method 1 (H_E)	40.6	6.9
Method 2 (H_Y)	29.1	11.9
Method 3 (H_A)	41.3	15.1

Note: Poverty line is $1 a person a day.

Inequality Measures and Their Decomposition

The main inequality measure used in this study is the Gini coefficient. But in the case study of Thailand we also use the mean log deviation, the Theil index, and a transform of the coefficient of variation. In their formulas below we use the following standard notation: y_i is the income of individual i, $i \in (1, 2, \ldots, n)$, n is the number of individuals in a given distribution, and $\mu(\mathbf{y})$ is the arithmetic mean of the distribution. The Gini is given by

$$(1) \qquad G = \frac{1}{2n^2\mu(y)} \sum_{i=1}^{n} \sum_{j=1}^{n} |y_i - y_j|$$

The other three measures are all members of the generalized entropy class of inequality indexes, which satisfy a number of desirable properties such as symmetry, population replication, scale invariance, and decomposability (see Cowell 1995 for details). The general formula for the parametric class is given by

$$(2) \qquad E(\alpha) = \frac{1}{\alpha^2 - \alpha} \left[\frac{1}{n} \sum_{i=1}^{n} \left(\frac{y_i}{\mu(y)} \right)^\alpha - 1 \right].$$

Using l'Hopital's rule one can obtain $E(0)$, the mean log deviation:

$$(3) \qquad E(0) = \frac{1}{n} \sum_{i=1}^{n} \log \left(\frac{\mu(y)}{y_i} \right).$$

Similarly, the Theil index corresponds to $E(1)$, which is given by

$$(4) \qquad E(1) = \frac{1}{n} \sum_{i=1}^{n} \frac{y_i}{\mu(y)} \log \left(\frac{y_i}{\mu(y)} \right).$$

The fourth measure we have employed is $E(2)$, which can be expressed as half of the square of the coefficient of variation:

$$(5) \qquad E(2) = \frac{1}{2n\mu(y)^2} \sum_{i=1}^{n} [y_i - \mu(y)]^2.$$

Any of the last three indexes, or indeed any member of the generalized entropy class given by equation 2, can be decomposed into between-group and within-group inequality components. Let $\Pi(k)$ be a partition of the population into k subgroups, indexed by j; $\mu(y)_j$ be the mean income in subgroup j; $E(\alpha)_j$ be the inequality measured for the population in subgroup j; $f_j = n_j/n$ be the population share of subgroup j; and

$v_j = \dfrac{n_j \mu(y)_j}{n\mu(y)}$ be the income share of subgroup j. If we define the between-group component E_B as $E_B = \dfrac{1}{\alpha^2 - \alpha}\left[\sum\limits_{j=1}^{k} f_j \left(\dfrac{\mu(y)_j}{\mu(y)}\right)^\alpha - 1\right]$

and the within-group component E_W as $E_W = \sum\limits_{j=1}^{k} w_j E(\alpha)_j$, where the

weights are given by $w_j = v_j^\alpha f_j^{1-\alpha}$, then Cowell and Jenkins (1995) show that overall inequality E can be written simply as $E = E_B + E_W$.[23] The share of inequality explained by a given partition Π for a specific generalized entropy measure E, reported in table 4.4, is simply $R_B(\Pi) = E_B(\Pi)/E$.

While these static decompositions shed some light on the structure of inequality at a given point in time, a different methodology is required to decompose the total change in inequality over a period into its three component effects: that due to changes in group population shares, that due to changes in relative mean income across groups, and that due to residual changes in within-group inequality. Mookherjee and Shorrocks (1982) have shown that the overall change in E(0) can be approximated by

(6) $\Delta E(0) \cong \sum\limits_{j=1}^{k} \overline{E(0)}_j \Delta f_j + \sum\limits_{j=1}^{k} [\overline{\lambda_j - \log(\lambda_j)}]\Delta f_j +$ (a + b)

$\sum\limits_{j=1}^{k} (\overline{v}_j - \overline{f}_j) \Delta \log \left(\mu(y)_j\right) +$ (c)

$\sum\limits_{j=1}^{k} \overline{f}_j \Delta E(0)_j$ (d)

where $\Delta x := x(t+1) - x(t)$ is the difference operator; an overbar indicates a simple average of the values of the variable at t and at $t+1$; and $\lambda_j = \mu(y)_j/\mu(y)$ is the ratio of group mean to overall mean.

The decomposition has four additive terms: a, b, c, and d. The sum of a and b gives the population share effect, c is the relative mean income effect, and d is the unexplained effect. After both sides are divided by $\Delta E(0)/100$, their values are entered in table 4.5 for the indicated partitions and time intervals.

Appendix B
Poverty Profile Tables and Figures

Table B.1 Thailand: Poverty Measures by Region, 1988, 1990, and 1992
(percent)

Region	Head-count index			Poverty gap index			Poverty severity index		
	1988	*1990*	*1992*	*1988*	*1990*	*1992*	*1988*	*1990*	*1992*
North	20.66	16.61	13.60	5.75	4.25	3.73	2.27	1.65	1.52
Northeast	34.51	28.27	22.31	10.55	7.48	5.59	4.49	2.97	2.08
Central	15.96	12.92	6.04	4.55	3.82	1.52	1.83	1.69	0.62
South	21.47	17.55	11.82	6.16	4.57	3.72	2.53	1.81	1.60
Bangkok	2.92	2.04	1.12	0.84	0.69	0.49	0.40	0.34	0.31
Bangkok vicinity	6.50	2.81	1.25	1.56	0.81	0.47	0.67	0.32	0.24
National	22.23	17.97	13.13	6.54	4.81	3.48	2.74	1.94	1.38

Source: World Bank 1996d, p. 7.

Table B.2   Indonesia: Distribution of Poverty by Province, 1990
(percent)

Province	Head-count		Share of population
	Index	Contribution to total	
Sumatra	15.7	16.4	20.5
Aceh	11.5	1.1	1.9
North Sumatra	12.1	3.6	5.8
West Sumatra	13.4	1.5	2.3
Riau	13.1	1.2	1.8
South Sumatra	14.6	2.6	3.5
Lampung	28.2	4.9	3.4
Other[a]	16.1	1.5	1.8
Java and Bali	19.3	61.6	62.5
Jakarta	1.3	0.3	4.6
West Java	17.6	17.9	19.9
Central Java	24.7	20.4	16.2
Yogyakarta	17.2	1.5	1.7
East Java	21.8	20.5	18.5
Bali	12.2	1.0	1.6
Kalimantan	20.3	5.3	5.1
West Kalimantan	33.8	3.2	1.8
South Kalimantan	8.7	0.7	1.5
Other[b]	16.0	1.5	1.8
Sulawesi	23.1	8.4	7.1
North Sulawesi	18.8	1.4	1.4
South Sulawesi	23.1	4.7	4.0
Other[c]	26.6	2.3	1.7
Eastern islands	34.9	8.5	4.8
West Nusa Tenggara	27.6	2.7	1.9
East Nusa Tenggara	45.6	4.3	1.9
Other[d]	29.0	1.5	1.0
National	19.6	100	100

a. Includes Jambi and Bengkulu.
b. Includes central and east Kalimantan.
c. Includes central and southeast Sulawesi.
d. Includes Maluku, excludes east Timor and Irian Jaya.
Source: World Bank 1993b, p. 10.

Table B.3 China: Distribution of Poverty by Province, 1989
(percent)

Province	Head-count index	
	National poverty line	*Provincial poverty line*
North		
Beijing	0.2	0.1
Tianjin	0.4	0.4
Hebei	13.0	11.7
Henan	16.5	15.2
Shandong	6.8	5.9
Northeast		
Liaoning	8.0	7.1
Jilin	12.2	10.7
Heilongjiang	18.3	17.9
Northwest		
Inner Mongolia	23.5	20.8
Shanxi	17.4	14.8
Shaanxi	20.3	18.4
Ningxia	18.9	18.4
Gansu	34.2	30.4
Qinghai	23.7	21.8
Xinjiang	18.7	17.6
Yangtze River		
Shanghai	0.0	0.0
Jiangsu	3.4	3.6
Zhejiang	2.0	2.3
Anhui	7.7	8.3
Jiangxi	5.0	6.4
Hubei	6.0	7.0
Hunan	6.2	7.7
South		
Fujian	1.8	2.1
Guangdong	0.9	1.1
Hainan	3.3	3.8
Southwest		
Guangxi	15.4	18.1
Sichuan	11.2	11.2
Guizhou	17.8	17.4
Yunnan	19.0	18.3
National	11.3	11.3

Note: The head-count index refers to the percentage of households in poverty.
Source: World Bank 1992, p. 142.

Table B.4 Papua New Guinea: Poverty Measures by Region, 1996
(percent)

	Head-count	
Region	Index	Contribution to total
National capital district	22.1	3.4
Papuan, South Coast	33.7	14.2
Highlands	31.8	36.0
Momase, North Coast	44.7	36.7
New Guinea islands	33.3	9.7
National	35.4	100.0
Urban	13.5	5.8
Rural	39.4	94.2

Source: Gibson and Rozelle 1997.

Table B.5 Vietnam: Poverty Measures by Region, 1992–93

	Head-count	
Region	Index	Contribution to total
Northern Uplands	66.3	18.9
Red River Delta	52.7	20.7
North Central	77.2	18.0
Central Coast	55.9	12.1
Central Highlands	66.8	3.9
Southeast	33.7	7.7
Mekong Delta	46.0	18.8
National	54.9	100.0
Urban	29.9	10.9
Rural	61.1	89.1

Source: Dollar and Glewwe forthcoming.

| Poverty gap | | Poverty severity | | |
Index	Contribution to total	Index	Contribution to total	Share of total population
5.8	2.8	2.2	2.4	5.5
12.5	16.4	5.9	17.2	14.9
9.8	34.6	4.3	34.0	40.1
14.0	36.0	6.3	36.4	29.2
11.2	10.1	4.9	10.0	10.3
11.3	100.0	5.1	100.0	100.0
3.4	4.5	1.1	3.3	15.1
12.8	95.5	5.8	96.7	84.9

| Poverty gap | | Poverty severity | | |
Index	Contribution to total	Index	Contribution to total	Share of total population
21.0	19.2	8.7	19.2	15.6
14.7	18.7	5.4	16.3	21.6
26.3	19.8	11.3	20.3	12.8
19.0	13.3	9.1	15.2	11.9
23.1	4.3	10.8	4.8	3.2
9.9	7.3	4.1	7.2	12.6
13.3	17.4	5.4	16.9	22.4
17.0	100.0	7.1	100.0	100.0
8.5	10.0	3.4	9.5	19.9
19.1	90.0	8.0	90.5	80.1

Table B.6 Philippines: Distribution of Poverty by Region, 1991
(percent)

| | Head-count | | Share of population |
Province	Index	Contribution to total	
National capital region	15.4	4.5	14.4
Ilocos	61.0	7.1	5.8
Cagayan Valley	58.2	4.6	3.9
Central Luzon	38.4	8.0	10.4
Southern Tagalog	48.8	13.4	13.7
Bicol	67.9	10.0	7.3
Western Visayas	52.7	9.8	9.3
Central Visayas	57.7	8.5	7.3
Eastern Visayas	58.6	6.4	5.4
Western Mindanao	61.3	5.1	4.1
Northern Mindanao	64.4	7.8	6.1
Southern Mindanao	59.7	8.6	7.2
Central Mindanao	63.9	4.2	3.2
Cordillera administrative region	49.1	2.0	2.0
National	49.7	100	100

Source: Deolalikar 1996.

Table B.7 Lao PDR: Poverty Measures by Region, 1992–93
(percent)

| | Head-count index | | | Poverty gap index | | | Poverty severity index | | |
Region	Rural	Urban	Total	Rural	Urban	Total	Rural	Urban	Total
North	52.7	16.0	46.4	12.9	2.5	11.1	4.5	0.6	3.8
Center	46.9	25.7	40.4	11.8	6.0	10.0	4.3	1.7	3.5
South	66.2	28.8	59.8	22.4	1.7	18.8	10.1	0.2	8.4
National	53.0	23.9	46.1	14.4	4.5	12.1	5.6	1.2	4.6

Source: World Bank 1995a, p. 6.

Poverty and Education of Household Head

Table B.8 Thailand: Poverty Incidence and Education of Household Head, 1992
(percent)

Education of household head	Head-count	
	Index	Contribution to total
No formal education	20.6	16.3
Primary	14.5	81.8
Secondary	3.0	1.7
Vocational	0.4	0.1
University	0.0	0.0
National	13.1	100.0

Source: Krongkaew 1996.

Table B.9 Philippines: Poverty Incidence and Education of Household Head, 1991
(percent)

Education of household head	Head-count	
	Index	Contribution to total
No formal education	72.3	5.6
Grades 1–5	67.9	35.0
Elementary graduate	60.5	31.1
High school, 1–3 years	52.7	12.3
High school graduate	35.4	12.0
College undergraduate	18.5	3.2
College graduate	6.0	1.0
National	49.7	100.0

Source: Deolalikar 1996.

Table B.10 Papua New Guinea: Poverty Measures by Education of Household Head, 1996
(percent)

Education of household head	Head-count		Poverty gap	
	Index	Contribution to total	Index	Contribution to total
No formal education	47.2	50.6	15.4	51.7
Less than grade 6	39.3	23.3	13.1	24.3
Primary (grade 6)	29.6	14.1	9.1	13.7
High school (grades 7–12)	16.0	4.9	4.5	4.3
Vocational	22.7	7.1	6.3	6.1
University	0.0	0.0	0.0	0.0
National	35.4	100.0	11.3	100.0

Source: Gibson and Rozelle 1997.

Table B.11 Lao PDR: Poverty Incidence and Education of Household Head, 1992–93
(percent)

Education of household head	Head-count index
No formal education	57.3
Primary	42.0
Lower secondary	33.8
Upper secondary	15.1
Technical college	26.3
University	0.0

Source: World Bank 1995a, p. 11.

Table B.12 Vietnam: Poverty Incidence and Education of Household Head, 1992–93
(percent)

Education of household head	Head-count	
	Index	Contribution to total
No formal education	67.5	14.7
Primary	56.9	38.9
Lower secondary	56.9	34.7
Upper secondary	43.6	9.8
Technical college	30.6	1.4
University	14.4	0.6
National	54.9	100.0

Source: Dollar and Glewwe forthcoming.

| | Poverty severity | | |
Index	Contribution to total	Share of total population
7.1	53.4	38.0
6.2	25.7	21.0
3.7	12.5	16.9
1.6	3.4	10.8
2.3	5.1	11.1
0.0	0.0	2.1
5.1	100.0	100.0

Poverty and Occupation of Household Head

Table B.13 Thailand: Poverty Measures by Occupation of Household Head, 1992
(percent)

| Occupation of household head | Head-count | | Share of population |
	Index	Contribution to total	
Professional/technical	0.7	0.2	3.7
Executive	0.0	0.0	1.0
Clerical	0.3	0.1	2.2
Sales	2.4	1.4	7.5
Service	2.2	0.6	3.8
Agriculture	20.1	76.6	50.0
Laborer	4.0	4.4	14.5
Inactive	12.7	16.7	17.2
National	13.1	100.0	100.0

Source: Krongkaew 1996.

Table B.14 Indonesia: Changes in the Sectoral Structure of Poverty, 1990 and 1993

Primary income source	Population share[a]		Head-count index		Contribution to national poverty[a]		Reduction due to sectoral gains[a]
	1990	1993	1990	1993	1990	1993	
Farming							
Laborer/employee	9.1	8.0					
Urban	1.2	1.1	23.1	20.2	1.5	1.8	0.6
Rural	7.9	6.9	32.4	25.3	13.2	13.6	8.8
Self-employed	42.4	37.9					
Urban	2.1	1.9	20.3	13.8	2.1	2.0	2.1
Rural	40.3	36.0	27.3	20.7	55.5	56.5	41.7
Mining							
Laborer/employee	0.8	0.8					
Urban	0.4	0.4	8.6	1.7	0.2	0.1	0.4
Rural	0.4	0.4	10.4	12.6	0.2	0.3	−0.1
Industry							
Laborer/employee	5.2	6.0					
Urban	3.2	3.4	10.5	4.0	1.7	1.1	3.3
Rural	2.0	2.6	15.1	10.3	1.5	2.1	1.5
Self-employed	2.5	2.7					
Urban	0.7	0.7	14.6	3.8	0.5	0.2	1.2
Rural	1.8	2.0	25.2	16.9	2.3	2.6	2.3
Construction							
Laborer/employee	4.0	4.8					
Urban	1.9	2.3	15.3	6.6	1.5	1.2	2.6
Rural	2.1	2.5	17.3	12.4	1.8	2.4	1.6
Self-employed	0.5	0.6					
Urban	0.3	0.3	11.0	7.5	0.2	0.2	0.2
Rural	0.2	0.3	16.5	7.5	0.2	0.2	0.3
Trade							
Laborer/employee	1.7	2.2					
Urban	1.3	1.6	7.3	1.9	0.5	0.2	1.0
Rural	0.4	0.6	16.1	8.1	0.3	0.4	0.5
Self-employed	12.5	13.3					
Urban	5.6	6.4	9.3	5.5	2.7	2.8	3.3
Rural	6.9	6.9	14.7	7.8	5.2	4.2	7.4

Table B.14 (continued)

Primary income source	Population share[a] 1990	Population share[a] 1993	Head-count index 1990	Head-count index 1993	Contribution to national poverty[a] 1990	Contribution to national poverty[a] 1993	Reduction due to sectoral gains[a]
Transportation							
Laborer/employee	2.5	2.8					
Urban	1.5	1.8	6.8	3.6	0.5	0.5	0.7
Rural	1.0	1.0	12.4	9.7	0.6	0.8	0.4
Self-employed	2.8	3.1					
Urban	1.4	1.6	18.8	8.4	1.4	1.0	2.3
Rural	1.4	1.5	14.2	8.1	1.0	1.0	1.4
Finance							
Laborer/employee	0.8	1.1					
Urban	0.7	0.9	1.1	0.4	0.0	0.0	0.1
Rural	0.1	0.2	6.7	4.3	0.0	0.1	0.1
Services							
Laborer/employee	12.3	13.3					
Urban	6.9	7.8	4.1	2.0	1.4	1.2	11.4
Rural	5.4	5.5	6.6	4.2	1.8	1.8	2.0
Self-employed	2.2	2.5					
Urban	1.3	1.4	12.6	5.5	0.8	0.6	1.4
Rural	0.9	1.1	17.9	8.0	0.8	0.7	1.4
All Indonesia			19.2	12.6			
Population shifts							12.0
Interaction effects							−0.3

Note: Farming includes farming, husbandry, hunting, and fishing. Mining includes mining and excavating. Industry includes industrial processing. Trade includes wholesale, retail, restaurant, and hotel. Transportation includes transportation, warehousing, and communications. Finance includes finance, insurance, office rental, and office services. Services include community services, social services, and personal services.

a. Components do not add up to 100 percent because of rounding and because several sectors were omitted due to small sample sizes.

Source: Mason and Baptist 1996.

Table B.15 Vietnam: Poverty Measures by Occupation of Household Head, 1992–93
(percent)

	Head-count	
Occupation of household head	Index	Contribution to total
White collar	25.3	2.1
Sales/service	30.4	4.5
Farming	64.5	75.9
Production	42.2	8.4
Other	50.4	0.9
Retired	39.2	4.6
Other (not working)	45.7	3.5
National	54.9	100.0

Source: Dollar and Glewwe forthcoming.

Table B.16 Philippines: Poverty Measures by Occupation of Household Head, 1991
(percent)

Occupation of household head	Head-count index	Poverty gap index	Poverty severity index	Share of total poor
Professional, technical, and related	31.1	10.4	4.7	3.4
Administrative, executive, and managerial	6.8	1.6	0.5	0.2
Clerical and related	11.9	3.3	1.3	0.6
Sales	31.0	9.1	3.7	4.9
Service	34.4	10.2	4.2	3.3
Agriculture, animal husbandry, forestry fishing, hunting	70.7	26.3	12.3	60.3
Production and related, transport, and equipment	43.3	12.9	5.3	19.4
Other	29.8	8.7	3.5	7.8
National	49.7	17.0	7.7	100.0

Source: Deolalikar 1996.

| Poverty gap | | Poverty severity | | |
Index	Contribution to total	Index	Contribution to total	Share of total population
5.9	1.6	2.0	1.3	4.6
7.4	3.5	2.6	3.0	8.1
20.5	77.7	8.7	79.2	64.7
12.4	7.9	4.9	7.5	10.9
21.6	1.2	11.3	1.5	1.0
12.1	4.6	4.6	4.2	6.5
13.7	3.4	5.6	3.3	4.2
17.0	100.0	7.1	100.0	100.0

Table B.17 Lao PDR: Poverty Measures by Activity Status of Household Head, 1992–93

(percent)

Activity status/ Occupation of household head	Head-count index	Poverty gap index
Farming	52.4	14.1
Self-employment and unpaid family labor	14.0	2.9
Government employment	24.5	4.8
Private sector employment	40.7	9.7
Retired/sick/elderly	24.6	5.7
Other (student, housekeeper, unemployed)	2.1	0.6

Source: World Bank 1995a, p. 105.

Regional Poverty Profiles

Figure B.1 Thailand: Poverty by Region, 1992

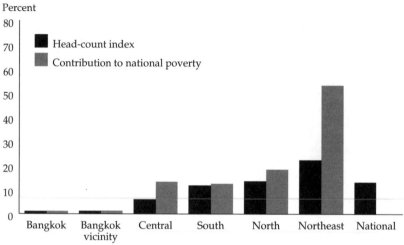

Source: Table B.1.

Figure B.2 Indonesia: Poverty by Province, 1990

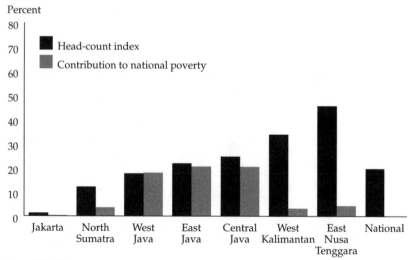

Source: Table B.2.

Figure B.3   China: Poverty by Province, 1989

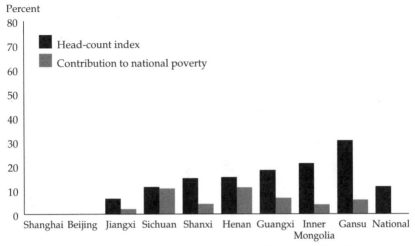

Note: Contribution to national poverty was calculated using population shares from *China Statistical Yearbook 1990.*
Source: Table B.3.

Figure B.4 Papua New Guinea: Poverty by Region, 1996

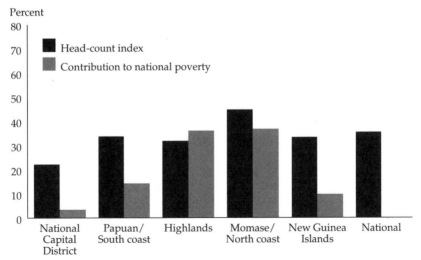

Source: Table B.4.

Figure B.5 Vietnam: Poverty by Region, 1992–93

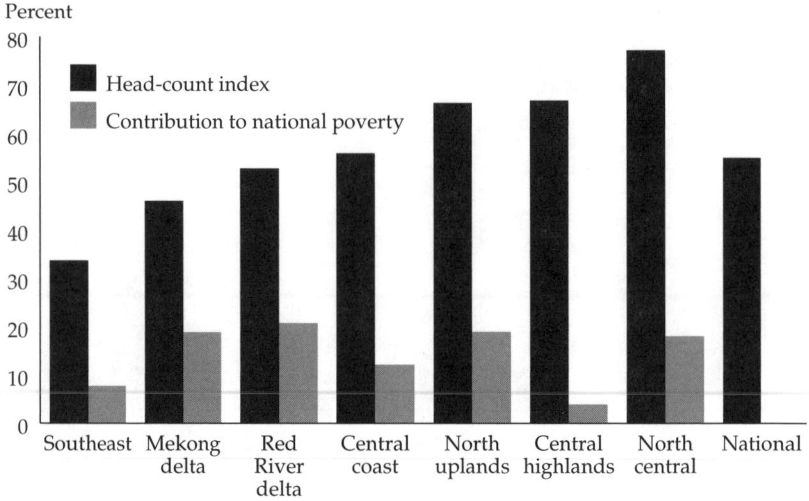

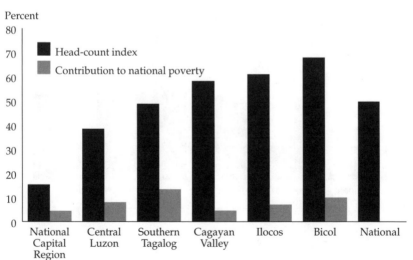

Source: Table B.5.

Figure B.6 Philippines: Poverty by Region, 1991

Source: Table B.6.

Figure B.7 Lao PDR: Poverty by Region, 1992–93

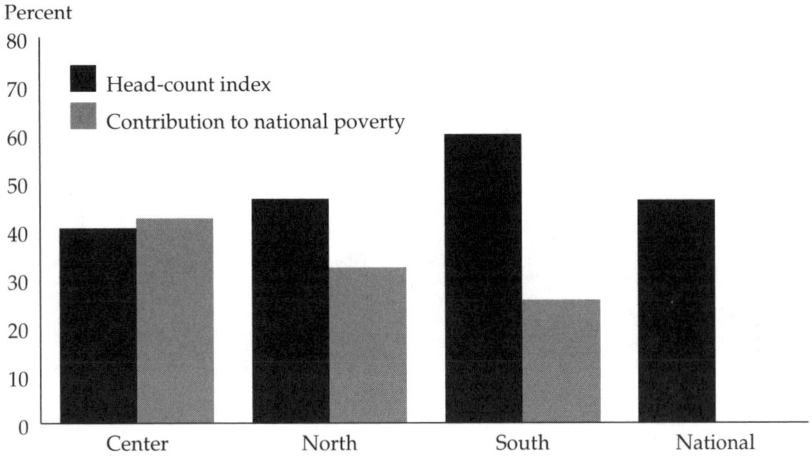

Percent

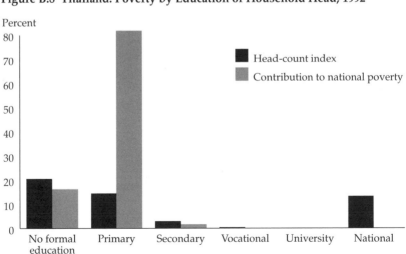

Source: Table B.7.

Poverty and Education of Household Head

Figure B.8 Thailand: Poverty by Education of Household Head, 1992

Percent

Source: Table B.8.

Figure B.9 Philippines: Poverty by Education of Household Head, 1991

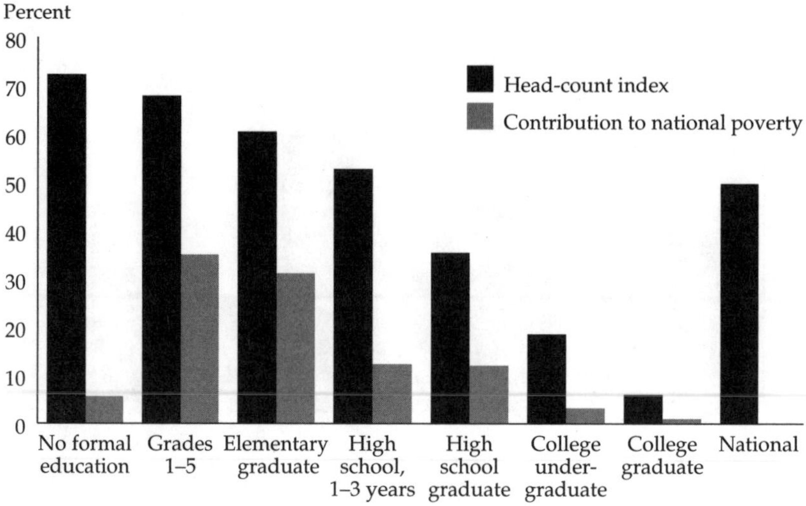

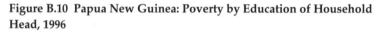

Percent

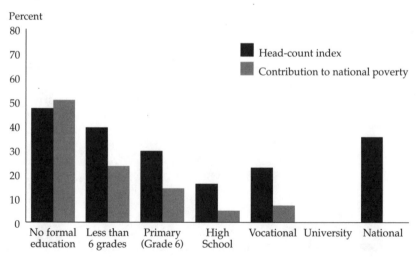

Source: Table B.9.

Figure B.10 Papua New Guinea: Poverty by Education of Household Head, 1996

Percent

Source: Table B.10.

Figure B.11 Lao PDR: Poverty by Education of Household Head, 1992–93

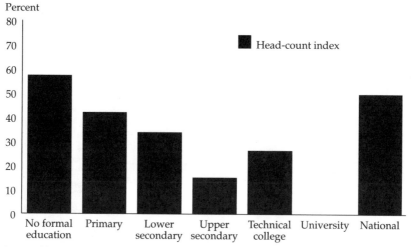

Source: Table B.11.

Figure B.12 Vietnam: Poverty by Education of Household Head, 1992–93

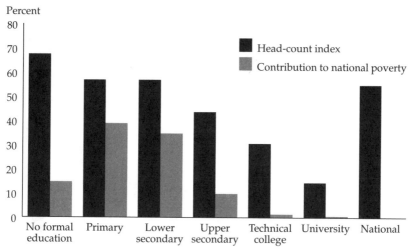

Source: Table B.12.

Poverty and Occupation of Household Head

Figure B.13 Thailand: Poverty by Occupation of Household Head, 1992

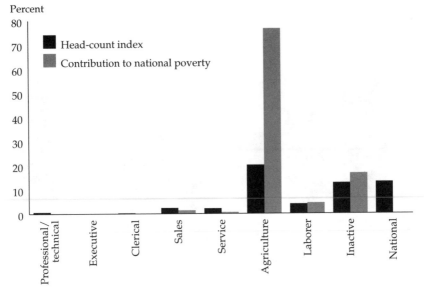

Source: Table B.13.

Figure B.14 Vietnam: Poverty by Occupation of Household Head, 1992–93

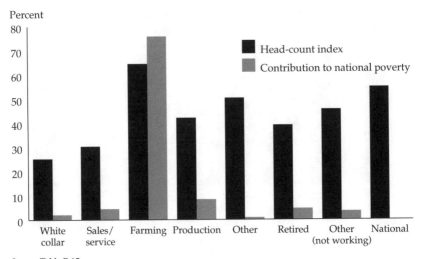

Source: Table B.15.

Figure B.15 Philippines: Poverty by Occupation of Household Head, 1991

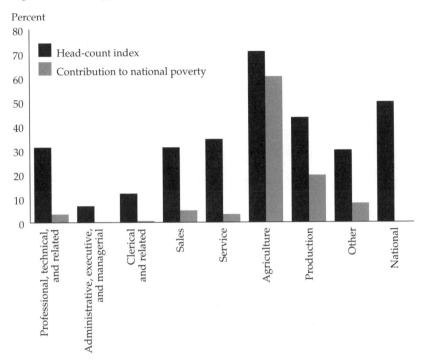

Source: Table B.16.

Appendix C
Poverty Profile for Thailand, 1975–92

Table C.1 Thailand: Poverty by Location and Region, 1975 and 1992
(percent)

| | | 1975 | |
| | | Head-count | |
	Population share	Index	Contribution to total
National	100.0	41.80	100.0
Location			
Urban	14.00	9.52	3.20
Semiurban	13.20	25.84	8.15
Rural	72.80	50.91	88.66
Region			
North	20.95	48.00	24.06
Urban	1.42	11.35	0.39
Semiurban	2.42	37.07	2.15
Rural	17.10	52.60	21.52
Northeast	35.13	59.49	50.00
Urban	1.70	13.96	0.57
Semiurban	3.35	36.02	2.89
Rural	30.08	64.68	46.55
Central	18.53	21.30	9.44
Urban	1.48	7.29	0.26
Semiurban	3.06	15.20	1.11
Rural	13.98	24.12	8.07
South	12.66	43.33	13.12
Urban	1.59	16.73	0.64
Semiurban	1.21	20.92	0.61
Rural	9.85	50.38	11.87
Bangkok	12.74	11.11	3.38

Source: Authors' calculations from the 1975 and 1992 Socioeconomic Surveys.

| | 1992 | |
| Population | Head-count | |
share	Index	Contribution to total
100.0	15.69	100.0
18.85	1.00	1.21
9.23	7.51	4.42
71.91	20.59	94.37
19.15	17.04	20.80
1.62	0.72	0.07
2.07	5.16	0.68
15.47	20.33	20.05
34.28	27.18	59.39
1.56	4.93	0.49
2.52	15.99	2.57
30.20	29.26	56.34
18.44	5.76	6.77
2.03	0.05	0.01
2.79	3.35	0.60
13.62	7.10	6.17
13.37	14.84	12.64
1.81	3.70	0.43
0.90	8.00	0.46
10.65	17.31	11.75
14.77	0.42	0.40

Table C.2 Thailand: Poverty by Socioeconomic Class, 1975–92
(percent)

| | 1975 | | |
| | | Head-count | |
	Population share	Index	Contribution to total
National	100.0	41.80	100.0
Socioeconomic class			
Farm operator owning land(rais)	43.34	54.63	56.74
Less than 2	0.54	60.71	0.79
2–4	2.58	61.25	3.79
5–9	6.88	64.76	10.68
10–19	12.97	63.10	19.62
20–39	12.67	52.17	15.84
40 or more	7.69	32.67	6.02
Farm operators renting land (rais)	10.75	51.03	13.15
Less than 5	1.16	74.91	2.07
5–19	4.40	62.71	6.62
20 or more	5.19	35.82	4.46
Fishing and forestry	2.02	44.11	2.13
Entrepreneurs, trade, and industry	14.59	19.93	6.97
With paid workers	1.42	3.50	0.12
Without paid workers	13.18	21.70	6.85
Professional, technical, and managerial	3.83	4.57	0.42
Self-employed	0.15	0.00	0.00
Employed by others	3.68	4.76	0.42
Laborers			
Farm	4.72	55.24	6.25
General	5.08	52.24	6.36
Other workers	12.95	19.23	5.97
Clerical, sales, and service	7.17	13.26	2.28
Production and construction	5.78	26.65	3.69
Economically inactive households	2.71	30.88	2.01
Receiving assistance or pensions	2.22	34.19	1.82
Receiving property income	0.49	15.91	0.19

Source: Authors' calculations from the 1975 and 1992 Socioeconomic Surveys.

	1992	
	Head-count	
Population share	Index	Contribution to total
100.0	15.69	100.0
34.88	25.68	57.09
0.23	15.25	0.23
1.58	26.20	2.64
5.56	30.67	10.87
11.62	27.44	20.33
11.11	26.42	18.72
4.77	14.18	4.32
4.75	18.98	5.74
0.37	26.17	0.62
2.28	25.37	3.70
2.09	10.73	1.43
0.70	13.38	0.60
14.52	2.77	2.57
3.14	0.91	0.18
11.38	3.29	2.38
5.37	0.15	0.05
0.19	4.10	0.05
5.17	0.00	0.00
5.99	36.17	13.81
3.94	23.42	5.89
22.40	6.19	8.84
11.12	2.62	1.85
11.27	9.72	6.98
7.46	11.39	5.42
6.52	12.47	5.18
0.94	3.91	0.23

Table C.3 Thailand: Poverty by Characteristics of Household Head, 1975–92

(percent)

| | 1975 | | |
| | Population share | Head-count | |
		Index	Contribution to total
National	100.0	41.80	100.0
Education of household head			
No formal education	21.83	46.64	24.35
Lower elementary	67.33	44.71	72.03
Upper elementary	2.84	24.61	1.67
Lower secondary	3.80	7.82	0.71
Upper secondary	0.52	3.19	0.04
Post-secondary[a]	0.80	0.49	0.01
Vocational training	0.53	4.17	0.05
Teacher training	0.82	1.48	0.03
Technical and advanced vocational	0.12	0.00	0.00
Other education or unknown	1.42	32.80	1.11
Sex of household head			
Male	86.57	42.98	89.01
Female	13.43	34.21	10.99
Age of household head (years)			
Less than 25	2.09	38.07	1.90
25–34	15.87	42.81	16.25
35–44	29.17	46.79	32.65
45–54	27.28	39.83	26.00
55–64	16.08	35.83	13.78
65 and older	9.51	41.37	9.42

a. Some university or more.
Source: Authors' calculations from the 1975 and 1992 Socioeconomic Surveys.

	1992	
Population share	Head-count	
	Index	*Contribution to total*
100.0	15.69	100.0
10.78	28.76	19.76
67.77	17.28	74.64
6.80	9.56	4.15
5.25	3.16	1.06
1.92	1.58	0.19
3.69	0.00	0.00
1.81	1.39	0.16
0.48	0.00	0.00
1.07	0.00	0.00
0.41	1.86	0.05
83.31	16.16	85.83
16.69	13.32	14.17
2.44	11.51	1.79
16.08	17.19	17.62
26.91	13.26	22.74
22.71	15.15	21.93
17.87	17.12	19.50
14.00	18.41	16.42

Appendix D
Growth Elasticities of Poverty
in Selected East Asian Countries

S tatements about "broad-based" growth are common, as are sugges-
tions that some episodes of economic expansion are friendlier to the
poor than others. In investigating the comparative effectiveness of
growth in reducing poverty, we found that the quantitative impact of
growth on poverty varied considerably within and across countries. The
variation in elasticities of the head-count index with respect to mean
consumption across and within countries is remarkable (table D.1).
During 1975–85 the Philippines exhibited the highest elasticity, followed
by Malaysia, Indonesia, and Thailand. Comparisons within countries
over time reveal similar variations. For a given growth rate, the rate of
poverty reduction in Indonesia during 1985–95 was more than twice
that of 1975–85. Thailand's turnaround was even more dramatic. While
poverty there rose during 1975–85 despite positive growth, the elasticity of poverty reduction was among the highest during 1985–92.

The elasticity depends on two key factors: the density function near
the poverty line, which determines the mass of people who cross it when
the distribution shifts to the right—ceteris paribus, the elasticity is greater
the greater is the density around the poverty line; and any changes in
inequality happening concurrently with growth—ceteris paribus, an
increase in inequality tends to reduce growth elasticity. Growth in which
the incomes of the poor rise faster than average would, through the second factor imply, higher elasticity. The discussion of policies in chapter 5
suggests a number of ways in which governments can seek to ensure that
the poor benefit at least as much as others from economic growth.

**Table D.1 Elasticity of the Head-count Index with Respect to Mean
Consumption**

Country	1975–85	1985–95
China (rural)	n.a.	−0.98
Indonesia	−0.66	−1.42
Malaysia	−0.95	n.a.
Philippines	−1.50	−0.67
Thailand	0.83	−1.86[a]

n.a. Not available.
a. 1985–92.
Source: Authors' calculations.

Notes

1. Due to lack of data, the Democratic People's Republic of Korea, Myanmar, and the Pacific islands are excluded from this study.

2. Unless otherwise specified, the symbol $ denotes U.S. dollars adjusted for purchasing power parity.

3. Naturally, this poverty line differs from the official lines used in individual countries. It happens to be close to that used domestically in some low-income economies, including Indonesia, but is above the official Chinese line, and below that adopted by many middle-income nations.

4. Cambodia would be a natural member of this group, but since the only household survey in 1993–94 used a truncated sampling frame, it is not representative of the whole country. For that reason we have not included it in table 2.1. As for the rest of the group, 1975 data available for these economies are too unreliable for analysis (see appendix A).

5. There are two closely related but distinct ways of profiling poverty across population subgroups. Let individuals be indexed by i. If the universe set (say, East Asia) is I, and there is a partition $\Pi = \{I_1, ..., I_k, ... I_K\}$ of K subgroups (say, countries), and the set of poor people is $P \subset I$, then group k's share of poverty is given by $Pr(i \in I_k \mid i \in P) = Pr(i \in P \cap I_k) / Pr(i \in P) = f_k H_k / H$, and group k's head-count is given by $Pr(i \in P \mid i \in I_k) = Pr(i \in P \cap I_k) / Pr(i \in I_k) = H_k$. Although some studies appear to confuse the two, it is clear that in any partition where the population shares f_k vary considerably the two concepts can lead to different results. Which one is the most appropriate guide for policy—for instance, targeting—is not a straightforward matter, and depends on the relative costs and benefits of targeting particular groups.

6. The Indonesian example illustrates the importance of clearly distinguishing between the subgroup head-count and the contribution-to-poverty concept of poverty profile. As the two types of bars in figure B.2 show, the ranking of Indonesia's regions would vary dramatically across those two measures.

7. There was more justification for the claim that the combination of high growth and reasonably low, stable inequality was unique to the region.

8. The observations in this data set are generally obtained from existing studies. Consequently, the set of comparable inequality measures is rather restricted. The Deininger-Squire data set contains only Gini coefficients and (top-to-bottom) quintile ratios. Though the Gini coefficient is not an ideal mea-

sure of inequality, it is far superior to the quintile ratio, which does not even satisfy the Pigou-Dalton transfer axiom. Thus in this section we rely on the Gini coefficient as our measure of inequality (for formulas, see appendix A).

9. As in the case of poverty, these comparisons ignore issues such as equivalence scales and differences in regional cost of living, which would have been addressed were the primary data available. In addition, we include Gini coefficients for both expenditure and income distributions. Since income distributions are generally more unequal than expenditure distributions, comparisons are only valid across indices for the same concept (for example, over time). Similarly, we include distributions per household and per individual, which, once again, are not strictly comparable. The figures merely indicate trends.

10. Increases in inequality may have been overstated by previous studies because of failures to value home production and imputed rents using appropriate local market prices, and to take into account regional price variations when deflating incomes (Ravallion and Chen 1997). Nevertheless, the latest evidence supports the view that increases have taken place.

11. It is possible to observe increases in inequality that leave poverty unchanged for a given level of average income. A mean-preserving spread originating from a transfer from an individual above the poverty line will increase inequality but not affect poverty.

12. These functions can take the form: $w = \sum_i f[u_i(y_i)]$ where $f' > 0$ and $f'' < 0$. Special cases include the Benthamite sum-of-utilities function ($f(U) = U$), provided individual utilities are concave in income, as well as the limiting case associated with John Rawls's "maxi-min" objective.

13. Although, as Deininger and Squire (1996) note, this result is based on data sets inferior in quality and coverage to their own.

14. An experiment was conducted in Indonesia on 8,000 households that were given short and long questionnaires on consumption. In the short form the number of food items was reduced from 218 to 15, and the number of nonfood items was reduced from 102 to 8. The distribution and the mean of food expenditures differed little between forms, but reported nonfood expenditures were 15 percent higher in the long questionnaire. However, other experiments report that the long form/short form ratio of food expenditures is 1.26 in Jamaica and 1.27 in El Salvador. Deaton and Grosh (1997) conclude that "as far as the level of disaggregation is concerned, we suspect that there is no free lunch here, and that drastic reductions in questionnaire length are likely to be risky and to lead to underestimation of the key consumption total." In Thailand in 1992, about 45 percent of household expenditures went toward food and nonalcoholic beverages; hence the extent of the bias applies to this part of consumption.

15. Nevertheless, recent analysis of the 1994 Socioeconomic Survey by Kakwani and Krongkaew (1997b) suggests that the upward trend in (income) inequality in Thailand may have leveled off after 1992. A detailed study of the latest poverty and inequality trends remains a subject for planned future research.

16. A very basic axiom, satisfied by most inequality measures in use anywhere, the Pigou-Dalton transfer axiom simply requires that the measure record an increase in inequality in response to an income transfer from a poorer to a richer person (a mean-preserving spread).

17. There is also a residual component that measures the change in poverty that can be attributed to the interaction between growth and redistribution components. If the mean expenditure or the Lorenz curve does not change over the decomposition period, the residual vanishes.

18. The experience of two neighboring countries, Thailand and Malaysia, provides an interesting contrast. The two countries had significantly different distributions of income in the mid-1970s. The Gini coefficient in Malaysia was about 50 percent, whereas in Thailand it was around 43 percent (both are income-based Gini coefficients). During the next fifteen years both countries grew at about the same rate, but the distribution of this growth across various sections of society followed different patterns. While the distribution of income in Malaysia improved (the Gini coefficient fell by about 5 percentage points), in Thailand it worsened (the Gini coefficient increased by more than 10 percentage points). By the late 1980s Thailand's income distribution had become more unequal than Malaysia's. Although a detailed causal analysis of this disparate experience is beyond the scope of this study, it appears that the New Economic Policy introduced by the Malaysian government in the early 1970s, which emphasized reducing poverty and improving social conditions through the expansion of primary education and health and eliminating racial differences in employment and asset ownership, helped improve income distribution.

19. The decompositions presented in table 5.1 apportion responsibility for given changes in poverty between growth and changes in the distribution. Another, complementary way of looking at the relationship between growth and changes in poverty is to investigate the impact of a given growth rate on the poverty head-count. The head-count elasticities with respect to mean consumption for rural China, Indonesia, Malaysia, the Philippines, and Thailand are presented in appendix table D.1.

20. Part of high (or low) saving performance is a consequence as much as a cause of high growth—countries can get on virtuous and vicious cycles (Schmidt-Hebbel and Servén 1997).

21. Other things being equal, an important caveat, refers to conditional convergence (Barro and Sala-i-Martin 1992). Without controlling for other determinants of growth, there is no evidence of unconditional convergence (Pritchett 1995).

22. POVCAL supports the following data types:

Type 1: p = cumulative proportion of population (ranked by the poverty indicator), L = cumulative proportion of expenditure held by that proportion of the population.

Type 2: q = proportion of population (as in p, but not cumulative), r = proportion of expenditure (as in L, but not cumulative).

Type 3: p (as in 1), r (as in 2).
Type 4:   q (as in 2), L (as in 1).
Type 5: $f(x)$ = percentage of population in a given class interval
           of incomes, X = mean expenditure of that class interval.
Type 6:   upper bound of a class interval, $f(x)$ (as in 5), X (as in 5).
Type 7:   upper bound of a class interval, p (as in 5), X (as in 5).
Type 8:   upper bound of a class interval, $f(x)$ (as in 5).

23. Cowell and Jenkins draw on earlier work by Bourguignon (1979), Cowell (1980), and Shorrocks (1980 and 1984).

Box Notes

Box 2.1

1. By using expenditure per capita we abstract from a number of issues in poverty analysis, such as intrahousehold economies of scale and differences in needs across age groups or gender, that are usually addressed by constructing adult equivalence scales. The effect of spatial price variations within any one country is also ignored.

Box 2.2

1. Data on poverty incidence and inequality prior to 1981 comparable to that presented in the box figure are not available. But it is widely believed that poverty incidence and inequality fell between 1978 and 1981 (see, for example, World Bank 1992). On the other hand, there is some uncertainty about the slowdown in poverty reduction in the mid- to late 1980s. Although in theory it is possible to explain the disconnect between overall GDP growth and per capita income growth in terms of retained earnings in the enterprise sector, there is some preliminary evidence that part of the measured slowdown may simply be due to undervaluation of consumption from own-farm production.

2. A production function–based accounting exercise by Lin (1992) suggests that about half the growth during 1978–84 came from enhanced application of inputs, especially fertilizers, as a result of price and production reforms. The household responsibility system also provided a big boost to productivity in the agriculture sector, accounting for nearly 47 percent of growth in crop output.

3. There also appears to be some appreciation of this view in Chinese policy circles. For example, the government recently extended land tenure to thirty years and proposed a freeze on the existing pattern of land distribution during the period of tenure. While the details on the implementation of the policy are not available, there already appears to be a revival of investment in the agriculture sector.

References

The word *processed* describes informally reproduced works that may not be commonly available through libraries.

ADB (Asian Development Bank). 1997. *Emerging Asia: Changes and Challenges.* Manila.

Aghion, Philippe, and Patrick Bolton. 1997. "A Theory of Trickle-Down Growth and Development." *Review of Economic Studies* 64: 151–72.

Agrawal, Nisha, and Michael Walton. 1996. "Women at Work in East Asia: Does Stellar Growth Meet the Needs of Women? Should Governments Do More?" World Bank, Poverty Reduction and Economic Management Network, Washington, D.C. Processed.

Ahuja, Vinod, and Deon Filmer. 1996. "Educational Attainment in Developing Countries: New Estimates and Projections Disaggregated by Gender." *Journal of Educational Planning and Administration* 3: 229–54.

Alesina, Alberto, and Dani Rodrik. 1994. "Distributive Politics and Economic Growth." *Quarterly Journal of Economics* 109 (2): 465–90.

Aoki, Masahiko, Hyung-Ki Kim, and Masahiro Okuno-Fujiwara, eds. 1996.*The Role of Government in East Asian Economic Development: Comparative Institutional Analysis.* New York: Oxford University Press.

Atkinson, Anthony B. 1970. "On the Measurement of Inequality." *Journal of Economic Theory* 2: 244–63.

Atkinson, Anthony B., and Joseph E. Stiglitz. 1980. *Lectures on Public Economics.* London: McGraw-Hill.

Banerjee, A. V., and A. F. Newman. 1991. "Risk-Bearing and the Theory of Income Distribution." *Review of Economic Studies* 58: 211–35.

———. 1993. "Occupational Choice and the Process of Development." *Journal of Political Economy* 101 (2): 274–98.

Barro, Robert J., and Xavier Sala-i-Martin. 1992. "Convergence." *Journal of Political Economy* 100 (2): 223–51.

Binswanger, Hans P., Klaus Deininger, and Gershon Feder. 1993. "Power, Distortions, Revolt, and Reform in Agricultural Land Relations." Policy Research Working Paper 1164. World Bank, Latin America and the Caribbean Technical Department, Washington, D.C.

Birdsall, Nancy, and Richard H. Sabot. 1993. "Virtuous Circles: Human Capital Growth and Equity in East Asia." Background paper for the *East Asian Miracle*. World Bank, Washington, D.C.

Bourguignon, François. 1979. "Decomposable Income Inequality Measures." *Econometrica* 47: 901–20.

Burgess, Robin. 1997. "Land, Welfare and Efficiency in Rural China." London School of Economics. Processed.

Burgess, Robin, and Juzhong Zhuang. 1996. "Dimensions of Gender Bias in Intrahousehold Allocation in Rural China." LSE-STICERD. London School of Economics. Processed.

Campos, Edgardo, and Hilton L. Root, eds. 1996. *The Key to the East Asian Miracle*. Washington, D.C.: Brookings Institution.

Chaudhuri, Shubham, and Martin Ravallion. 1994. "How Well Do Static Indicators Identify the Chronically Poor?" *Journal of Public Economics* 53: 367–94.

Choe, Chongwoo. 1996. "Incentive to Work versus Disincentive to Invest: The Case of China's Rural Reform, 1979–84." *Journal of Comparative Economics* 22: 242–66.

Cowell, F. A. 1980. "On the Structure of Additive Inequality Measures." *Review of Economic Studies* 47: 521–31.

———. 1995. *Measuring Inequality*. 2nd ed. Englewood Cliffs, N.J.: Prentice-Hall.

Cowell, F. A., and S. P. Jenkins. 1995. "How Much Inequality Can We Explain? A Methodology and an Application to the USA." *Economic Journal* 105: 421–30.

Crook, Frederick. 1994. "Seeds of Change." *China Business Review* (November–December): 20–26.

Datt, Gaurav, and Martin Ravallion. 1992. "Growth and Redistribution Components of Changes in Poverty Measures." *Journal of Development Economics* 38: 275–95.

Deaton, Angus. 1989. "Looking for Boy-Girl Discrimination in Household Expenditure Data." *The World Bank Economic Review* 3 (1): 1–15.

———. 1997. *The Analysis of Household Surveys: A Microeconometric Approach to Development Policy*. Baltimore, Md.: The Johns Hopkins University Press.

Deaton, Angus, and Margaret Grosh. 1997. "The Consumption Module in the Living Standards Measurement Study." World Bank, Development Research Group, Washington, D.C. Processed.

Deininger, Klaus, and Lyn Squire. 1996. "A New Data Set Measuring Income Inequality." *The World Bank Economic Review* 10 (3): 565–91.

Deolalikar, A. 1996. "Poverty and Income Distribution." Background paper for the World Bank's Philippines Poverty Assessment.

University of Washington, Seattle.

DGB (Directorate-General of Budget, Accounting, and Statistics). 1996. "Report on the Survey of Family Income and Expenditure in Taiwan Area of the Republic of China." Executive Yuan, Republic of China.

————. Various years. "Social Indicators in Taiwan Area of the Republic of China." Executive Yuan, Republic of China.

Dollar, David, and Paul Glewwe. Forthcoming. "Poverty and Inequality in the Early Reform Period." In David Dollar, Paul Glewwe, and Jennie Litvack, eds., *Household Welfare and Vietnam's Transition to a Market Economy*. Washington, D.C.: World Bank.

Dollar, David, and Jennie Litvack. Forthcoming. "Macroeconomic Reform and Poverty Reduction." In David Dollar, Paul Glewwe, and Jennie Litvack, eds., *Household Welfare and Vietnam's Transition to a Market Economy*. Washington, D.C.: World Bank.

Drèze, Jean, and Amartya K. Sen. 1989. *Hunger and Public Action*. Oxford: Clarendon Press.

Feder, Gershon, Lawrence J. Lau, Justin Yifu Lin, and Xiaopenf Luo. 1992. "The Determinants of Farm Investment and Residential Construction in Post-Reform China." *Economic Development and Cultural Change* 41 (October): 1–26.

Ferreira, F. H. G. 1995. "Roads to Equality: Wealth Distribution Dynamics with Public-Private Capital Complementarity." LSE-STICERD Discussion Paper TE/95/286. London School of Economics.

Ferreira, F. H. G., and J. A. Litchfield. 1996. "Growing Apart: Inequality and Poverty Trends in Brazil in the 1980s." LSE-STICERD Discussion Paper DARP/23. London School of Economics.

————. Forthcoming. "Education or Inflation? The Roles of Structural Factors and Macroeconomic Instability in Explaining Brazilian Inequality in the 1980s." LSE-STICERD Discussion Paper. London School of Economics.

Foster, J. E., J. Greer, and Erik Thorbecke. 1984. "A Class of Decomposable Poverty Indices." *Econometrica* 52: 761–66.

Galor, Oded, and Joseph Zeira. 1993. "Income Distribution and Macroeconomics." *Review of Economic Studies* 60: 35–52.

Gibson, John, and Scott Rozelle. 1997. "Results of the Household Survey Component of the 1996 Poverty Assessment for Papua New Guinea." University of Waikato, Hamilton, New Zealand. Processed.

Gunderson, Morley. 1989. "Male-Female Wage Differentials and Policy Responses." *Journal of Economic Literature* 27 (1): 46–72.

Howes, S. R. 1993. "Income Distribution: Measurement, Transition and Analysis of Urban China, 1981–1990." Ph.D. dissertation. London School of Economics.

Jitsuchon, S. 1990. "Alleviation of Rural Poverty in Thailand." ARTEP

Working Papers. International Labour Organization, New Delhi.

Johansen, Frida. 1993. *Poverty Reduction in East Asia: The Silent Revolution.* World Bank Discussion Paper 203. Washington, D.C.

Kakwani, Nanak. 1980. "On a Class of Poverty Measures." *Econometrica* 48: 437–46.

Kakwani, Nanak, and Medhi Krongkaew. 1996. "Defining and Measuring Poverty in Thailand." University of New South Wales, Sydney, Australia. Processed.

———. 1997a. "Poverty in Thailand: Defining, Measuring and Analyzing." National Economic and Social Development Board, Development Evaluation Division, Bangkok.

———. 1997b. "Some Good News on Poverty and Income Inequality." University of New South Wales, Sydney, Austrailia. Processed

Kim, D. I., and R. Topel. 1995. "Labor Markets and Economic Growth: Lessons from Korea's Industrialization, 1970–1990." In Richard B. Freeman and Lawrence F. Katz, eds., *Differences and Changes in Wage Structures.* Chicago, Ill.:University of Chicago Press.

Kraay, Aart. 1996. "A Resilient Residual: Accounting for China's Growth Performance in Light of the Asian Miracle." World Bank, Development Research Group, Washington, D.C. Processed.

Krongkaew, M. 1996. "Thailand: Poverty Assessment Update." Thammasat University, Bangkok. Processed.

Krongkaew, M., P. Tinakorn, and S. Suphachalasai. 1996. "Thailand." In M. G. Quibria, ed., *Rural Poverty in Developing Asia.* Vol. 2. Manila: Asian Development Bank.

Krugman, Paul. 1994. "Myth of Asia's Miracle." *Foreign Affairs* 73 (November–December): 62–78.

Kuznets, Simon. 1955. "Economic Growth and Income Inequality." *American Economic Review* 45: 1–28.

Lin, Justin Yifu. 1992. "Rural Reforms and Agricultural Growth in China." *American Economic Review* 82 (1): 34–51.

Mason, Andrew D., and Jacqueline Baptist. 1996. "How Important Are Labor Markets to the Welfare of the Poor in Indonesia?" Policy Research Working Paper 1665. World Bank, Poverty and Social Policy Department, Washington, D.C.

Meesook, Oey Astra. 1979. "Income, Consumption and Poverty in Thailand, 1962/63 to 1975/76." World Bank Staff Working Paper 364. Washington, D.C.

Meng, Xin. 1996. "The Economic Position of Women in East Asia." *Asian Pacific Economic Literature* 10 (May): 23–41.

Mookherjee, Dilip, and A. F. Shorrocks. 1982. "A Decomposition Analysis of the Trend in U.K. Income Inequality." *Economic Journal* 92: 886–902.

Oaxaca, Ronald. 1973. "Male-Female Wage Differentials in Urban Labor Markets." *International Economic Review* 14 (1): 693–709.

Park, Y-B., D. R. Ross, and R. H. Sabot. 1996. "Educational Expansion and the Inequality of Pay in Brazil and Korea." In Nancy Birdsall and Richard H. Sabot, eds., *Opportunity Foregone: Education in Brazil*. Baltimore, Md.: The Johns Hopkins University Press.

Persson, Torsten, and Guido Tabellini. 1994. "Is Inequality Harmful to Growth?" *American Economic Review* 84 (3): 600–21.

Pritchett, Lant. 1995. "Divergence, Big Time." Policy Research Working Paper 1522. World Bank, Office of the Vice President, Development Economics, Washington, D.C.

Prosterman, Roy L., Tim Hanstad, and Li Ping. 1996. "Can China Feed Itself?" *Scientific American* (November): 90–96.

Quisumbing, A. R., L. Haddad, and C. Pena. 1995. "Gender and Poverty: New Evidence from Ten Developing Countries." FCND Discussion Paper 9. International Food Policy Research Institute, Washington, D.C.

Ravallion, Martin. 1994. *Poverty Comparisons*. Fundamentals of Pure and Applied Economics, Vol. 56. Chur, Switzerland: Harwood Academic Press.

Ravallion, Martin, and Shaohua Chen. 1997. "A Note on the Measurement of Income Inequality in Post-Reform Rural China." World Bank, Development Research Group, Washington, D.C. Processed.

Ravallion, Martin, Gaurav Datt, and Dominique van de Walle. 1991. "Quantifying Absolute Poverty in the Developing World." *Review of Income and Wealth* 37 (December): 345–61.

Rueda-Sabater, E. J., and associates. 1985. "Poverty in Thailand: A Profile of Households and Villages." World Bank, Washington, D.C. Processed.

Saposnik, Rubin. 1981. "Rank-Dominance in Income Distribution." *Public Choice* 36: 147–51.

Sarel, Michael. Forthcoming. "Growth and Productivity in ASEAN Countries." IMF Working Paper. International Monetary Fund, Washington, D.C.

Sarvananthan, Muttukrishna. 1997. "Poverty and Inequality in Asia: A Survey of Recent Literature and Research Agenda." Indonesia Discussion Paper Series 6. World Bank, East Asia and the Pacific Region, Washington, D.C.

Schmidt-Hebbel, Klaus, and Luis Servén. 1997. *Saving across the World: Puzzles and Policies*. World Bank Discussion Paper 354. Washington, D.C.

Sen, Amartya K. 1976. "Poverty: An Ordinal Approach to Measurement." *Econometrica* 46: 437–46.

————. 1981. *Poverty and Famines: An Essay on Entitlement and Deprivation.* Oxford: Clarendon Press.

————. 1985. *Commodities and Capabilities.* Amsterdam: North-Holland.

Shorrocks, A.F. 1980. "The Class of Additively Decomposable Inequality Measures." *Econometrica* 48: 613–25.

————. 1984. "Inequality Decomposition by Population Subgroup." *Econometrica* 52: 1369–85.

SSB (State Statistical Bureau). Various years. *China Statistical Yearbook.* Beijing.

Summers, Robert, and Alan Heston. 1991. "The Penn World Table (Mark 5): An Expanded Set of International Comparisons 1950–1988." *Quarterly Journal of Economics* 106: 327–68.

Teranishi, Juro. 1996. "Sectoral Resource Transfer, Conflict and Macro-stability in Economic Development: A Comparative Analysis." In Masahiko Aoki, Hyung-Ki Kim, and Masahiro Okuno-Fujiwara, eds., *The Role of Government in East Asian Economic Development: Comparative Institutional Analysis.* New York: Oxford University Press.

Villaseñor, J., and B. C. Arnold. 1989. "Elliptical Lorenz Curves." *Journal of Econometrics* 40: 327–38.

van de Walle, Dominique, and Kimberly Nead. 1995. *Public Spending and the Poor: Theory and Evidence.* Baltimore, Md.: The John Hopkins University Press.

Wen, Guanzhong James. 1995. "The Land Tenure System and Its Saving and Investment Mechanism: The Case of Modern China." *Asian Economic Journal* 9 (3): 233–59.

Williamson, J., and B. Polak. 1990. "Poverty, Policy and Industrialization: Lessons from the Distant Past." Background paper for *World Development Report 1990.* World Bank, World Development Report Office, Washington, D.C.

World Bank. 1990a. *Indonesia: A Strategy for a Sustained Reduction in Poverty.* A World Bank Country Study. Washington D.C.

————. 1990b. *World Development Report: Poverty.* New York: Oxford University Press.

————. 1991. "Growth, Poverty Alleviation and Improved Income Distribution in Malaysia: Changing Focus of Government Policy Intervention." Report 8667-MA. Washington, D.C.

————. 1992. *China: Strategies for Reducing Poverty in the 1990s.* A World Bank Country Study. Washington, D.C.

————. 1993a. *The East Asian Miracle: Economic Growth and Public Policy.* New York: Oxford University Press.

————. 1993b. "Indonesia: Public Expenditures, Prices and the Poor." Report 11293-IND. Washington, D.C.

————. 1993c. "Thailand: Poverty Assessment." Report 11928-TH. Washington, D.C.

————. 1995a. "Lao PDR: A Social Development Assessment and Strategy." Report 13992-LA. Washington, D.C.

————. 1995b. "Viet Nam: Poverty Assessment and Strategy." Report 13442-VN. Washington, D.C.

————. 1996a. "Mongolia: Poverty Assessment in a Transition Economy." Report 15723-MOG. Washington, D.C.

————. 1996b. "Philippines: Strengthening Economic Resiliency." Report 15985-PH. Washington, D.C.

————. 1996c. *Poverty Reduction and the World Bank: Progress and Challenges in the 1990s.* Washington, D.C.

————. 1996d. "Thailand: Growth, Poverty and Income Distribution." Report 15689-TH. Washington, D.C.

————. 1996e. "Vietnam: Education Financing Sector Study." Report 15925-VN. Washington, D.C.

————. 1997a. "China Rising: Long Term Issues and Options in the 21st Century." Report 16643-CHA. Washington, D.C.

————. 1997b. Income Inequality in China." Report 16685-CHA. Washington, D.C.

————. 1997c. "Indonesia: Sustaining High Growth with Equity." Report 16433-IND. Washington, D.C.

————. 1997d. "Poverty and Income Distribution in a High-Growth Economy: Chile, 1987–1995." Report 16377-CH. Washington, D.C.

————. Forthcoming. "Indonesia: Suggested Priorities for Education." Washington, D.C.

Yao, Yang. 1995. "Institutional Arrangements, Tenure Insecurity and Agricultural Productivity in Post-Reform Rural China." University of Wisconsin, Department of Agricultural Economics. Madison.

Young, Alwyn. 1994. "The Tyranny of Numbers: Confronting the Statistical Realities of the East Asian Growth Experience" *Quarterly Journal of Economics* 110 (August): 641–80.